DISCOVER YOUR RICHES IN CHRIST

BY:
DR. LEE TURNER

FOREWORD BY:
DR. CHARLES R. SOLOMON
Author, *Handbook to Happiness*

Discover Your Riches In Christ

"The glorious riches of this mystery, which is Christ in you, the hope of glory" (Colossians 1:27).

ISBN 0978-1-7324042-5-0

Cover by
Gregg Bishop
Grafx Solutions
Phoenix, AZ

Dedication

To my wife, Mary, who has enriched my life by her love, light-heartedness, companionship and spiritual insights. Our joint-triumph through trials has given us a deep conviction that real joy comes not by changing our circumstances, but by resting in the unchanging sufficiency of Christ.

Her vibrant life is a transparent manifestation of Christ in all his beauty. She has not only been an infectious inspiration to me but also excited many to understand and appropriate the resurrected life of Christ.

DISCOVER YOUR RICHES IN CHRIST

Table of Contents

Introduction

A child's description of an elevator was, "I got into this little room and the upstairs came down." That could be a description of what happened when we received Christ as our personal savior. Heaven opened up and God emptied His dump truck of grace and gave us everything there was to give *in Christ.* He,

> *blessed us in heavenly realms with every spiritual blessing in Christ* (Ephesians 1:3).

The phrase *in Christ* or its related forms occurs 165 times in the 23 letters of Paul. However, in the book of Ephesians alone it occurs 31 times; and 40 times if you count indirect references. *In Christ* occurs ten times more than *Christ in us.* Yet I wonder how many believers have discovered the riches they have in Christ?

Paul starts the book of Ephesians by mentioning a few of the riches we have in Christ:

> *...who has blessed us in the heavenly realms with every spiritual blessing in Christ* (Ephesians 1:3).

> *For He chose us in Him before the creation of the world...* (v. 4).

> "*...predestined us to be adopted as His sons*" (v. 5).

In Him we have redemption through His blood, the forgiveness of sins... (v. 7).

In Him we were chosen... (v. 11)

And you also were included in Christ when you heard the word of truth, the gospel of your salvation. Having believed, you were marked in Him with a seal, the promised Holy Spirit for Himself (v. 13).

How great are these riches that we want to discover? Paul describes them as,

The riches of God's grace that He lavished on us with all wisdom and understanding (Ephesians 1:7-8).

They are unfathomable and inexhaustible. Paul spoke of God's greatness,

Oh, the depth of the riches both of the wisdom and knowledge of God! How unsearchable are His judgments and His ways past finding out (Romans 11:33).

Unsearchable in the Greek means *not tracked out.*

Immanuel Kant, commenting on the size of the universe said, *All the capability of human conception sinks exhausted.* In Christ, the creator and sustainer of the universe, has showered us with unsearchable riches. Paul speaks of them as,

The glorious riches of this mystery, which is Christ in you, the hope of glory (Colossians 1:27).

Paul exhausts his vocabulary describing them,

> *Now to Him who is able to do immeasurably more than all we ask or imagine, according to His power that is at work within us* (Ephesians 3:20).

In Christ, we have everything.

> *It is because of Him that you are in Christ Jesus, Who has become for us wisdom of God—that is our righteousness, holiness, and redemption* (1 Corinthians 1:30).

Why would God lavish all these blessings on us? Is it just so that we would feel good? No. It's not about us—it's all about God! He provided these riches so that He might be glorified in us. This theme is interspersed with these promises:

- *to the praise of His glorious grace* (verse 6);
- *in order that* (a purpose clause) *we, who were the first to hope in Christ, might be for the praise of His glory* (verse 12);
- *to the praise of His glory* (verse 14).

He gives believers these blessings that we might glorify Him in our lives.

After enumerating the riches that believers have in Christ, Paul said,

> *I pray also that the eyes of your heart (or understanding) may be enlightened in order that you may know the hope to which He has called you, the*

riches of His glorious inheritance in the saints, and His incomparably great power for us who believe. That power is like the working of His mighty strength (vv. 18-19).

Paul emphasized that these great truths must be more than intellectual knowledge. Head knowledge must become heart knowledge. The *eyes of our heart* must be *enlightened* so the *riches of His glorious inheritance* might become a reality in our innermost being.

When someone says, "I see it!" they mean they understand the reality of some truth. Something they knew intellectually suddenly gripped them and became a reality. It 'dawned' on them and they were illuminated and impacted by it.

Many believers understand that *Christ is in them* but fail to understand that they are also *in Christ.*

His Spirit is in us and our spirit is in Him. How can this be? Paul said,

But he who unites himself with the Lord is one with Him in spirit (1 Corinthians 6:17).

This is such a wonderful truth that Paul calls it,

The glorious riches of this mystery, which is Christ in you, the hope of glory (Colossians 1:27).

It is a *mystery.* We can't explain it, but we can believe it because God said it. If Christ can dwell in us through the Holy Spirit, then we can accept the fact that our spirit dwells in Him. Failure to grasp this great truth can rob believers from appropriating their riches in Christ.

We are told in 2 Peter 1:3 that

His divine power has given us everything we need for life and godliness.

The question is, "Why are many Christians emaciated spiritually and lacking power and purity in their lives?" We are told in verse 4,

Through these He has given us His very great and precious promises, so that through them we may participate in the divine nature and escape the corruption in the world caused by evil desires.

These *very great and precious promises* must be claimed. We must learn how to possess our possessions in Christ! May this book help you discover your riches in Christ.

The very next verse challenges us to *make every effort to add to your faith*, then lists different virtues.

God has given us unlimited resources,

For in Christ all the fullness of the Deity lives in bodily form and you have been given fullness in Christ (Colossians 2:9-10).

However, these inexhaustible resources are only *promises*, until we claim them and make them ours.

In the 18th century, some Colonists left Virginia and moved west in the mountains. For 20 years they were cut off from the outside world. They had not heard of the Revolutionary War, the establishment of the Republic, the policies of Congress, etc. When they were told of their new status they became American citizens in that hour by their knowledge as they had already been in fact.

Many believers are not aware of and have not appropriated the inexhaustible riches they have in Christ. I have entitled this book, *Discovering Your Riches in Christ*, because we want to examine a few of these precious jewels discovered in God's grace and claim them as our own.

In January 1983, a three-nation astronomy satellite soared into a 560-mile orbit above the earth and pointed its tracking antennae toward deep space. Almost at once, an avalanche of information poured into the computers at an English ground station. More than two hundred thousand new objects were soon spotted in the heavens, including twenty thousand galaxies in interstellar space. Astronomers couldn't believe their good fortune. Having convinced themselves of the universe's emptiness, the new treasures stunned them. Christians were delighted, but not surprised. God has created more in this world than can ever be investigated, studied, or understood.

The same can be said of this book; it will only be a mere reflection of *the unsearchable riches we have in Christ*.

CHRIST IN YOU, THE HOPE OF GLORY
Colossians 1:27b

Christ in you, The believer's hope;
Self in you can only cope.
Christ in you, The believer's power;
Self in you can only cower.

Christ in you—Life from the Cross;
Self in you is to suffer loss.
Christ in you permits revival;
Self in you portends survival.

Christ in you, Life to others; (2 Cor. 4:12)
Self in you, death to brothers.
Christ in you, glory to Him;
Self in you, the future's dim. (2 Cor. 5:10)

Christ in you, the Church's hope;
Self in charge, and it does mope.
Christ in you, the Church empowered;
With revival fires, blessings showered.

Christ in you, The hope of glory;
Self in you is another story!

C. R. Solomon
November 7, 2008

Chapter 1

IN CHRIST WE HAVE
ETERNAL LIFE — HIS LIFE

The greatest blessing we have in Christ is eternal life—which is Christ's life. At our first birth, we were born into Adam's family and not into the family of God. We can all trace our first birth lineage back through our parents, our grandparents, and their ancestors all the way back to Adam. We were in Adam when he sinned; and this made us sinners by birth,

> *Therefore, just as sin entered the world through one man, and death through sin, and in this way death came to all men, because all sinned* (Romans 5:12).

We were all born separated spiritually from God.

Since we are born spiritually dead, our greatest need is spiritual life. We received physical life, and psychological life, and a spirit which was dead to God by our human birth. This physical birth gave us only temporary human life. Unfortunately, every human will die. To escape this living death condition, we must be born again into a spiritual life by a spiritual rebirth,

> *God, Who is rich in mercy, made us alive with Christ, even when we were dead in transgression—it is by grace you have been saved* (Romans 2:4,5).

We are *made alive with Christ* through the new birth and have eternal life — which is the very life of Christ.

Eternal Life is Christ's Life

If someone asked you for a definition of eternal life, what would you say? Some might say, "It means I will live forever." They think of it as an extension of their life. A Biblical definition of eternal life is,

> *And this is the testimony, God has given us eternal life, and this life is in His Son. He who has the Son has life; he who doesn't have the Son of God does not have life* (1 John 5:11-12).

Only one person has eternal life, and that is God; therefore, eternal life is Christ's life.

In eternity past, He always existed,

> *In the beginning was the Word, and the Word was with God, and the Word was God, He was with God in the beginning* (John 1:1-2).

At a point in time, He came to earth and took on a human body,

> *The Word became flesh and made His dwelling among us* (v. 14).

But He lived in that body the same life He had always lived as God. He lived in a human body for about thirty-three years, then ended His earthly existence at the cross where He bore our sins. He died, was buried, raised, and returned to Heaven where He continues to live the same life He has always lived,

> *Jesus Christ is the same yesterday and today and forever* (Hebrews 13:8).

When we trust Christ as our personal savior we are taken out of Adam's life and placed into Christ's life at the cross,

> *Or don't you know that all of us who were baptized into Christ Jesus were baptized into His death? We were therefore buried with Him through baptism into death in order that, just as Christ was raised from the dead through the glory of the Father, we too may live a new life* (Romans 6:3-4).

The cross paid for our sins and reconciled us to God; but dead men need life! Believers now share in His resurrected life,

> *For if, when we were reconciled to Him through the death of His Son, how much more, having been reconciled, shall we be saved through* (or in) *His life!* (Romans 5:10).

Through Adam we were made sinners and through Christ we were made righteous,

> *For if, by the trespass of the one man,* (Adam) *death reigned through that one man, how much more will those who receive God's abundant provision of grace and of the gift of righteousness reign in life through the one man, Jesus Christ* (Romans 5:17).

We were taken out of the old life we inherited from Adam and put into Christ by the Spirit of God. In Christ *we now have a new identity,*

> *Therefore, if anyone is in Christ, he is a new creation, the old has gone, the new has come* (2 Corinthians 5:17).

Once we are in Christ, we are in an eternal existence—a life that is not based on time. Our new eternal life is not an extension of our life; it is entering into Christ's life—a life which spans the past as well as the future. This new life is traced back, not through our first ancestor, Adam, but back through Christ.

Being *in Christ* means being in Him eternally. We were chosen in Him before the foundation of the world,

> *For He chose us in Him before the creation of the world* (Ephesians 1:4).

And we are already seated with Him in the heavens,

> *And God raised us up with Christ and seated us with Him in the heavenly realms in Christ Jesus* (Ephesians 2:6).

Notice the repetition of the concept of *in Christ* occurs both in eternity past and being seated with Him in Heaven now.

We not only have the eternal life of Christ now and throughout eternity, but we also have a new past! All of our sins were canceled on the cross—our guilt is gone. We are free to enjoy our present life without the emotional damage of our past.

Alan Redpath wrote,

> *The deepest, most real, and most wonderful meaning of Calvary is that not only did Jesus die there for my sins, but I died with Him and in Him. Without a real spiritual revelation to your heart of this, you will never be a victorious Christian.*
> —*Victorious Christian Living*, page 68.

We are not only totally forgiven, forever, but, more startlingly, we are a completely new person forever! An ugly worm goes through a transformation (Greek word metamorphize) in a cocoon and emerges a beautiful butterfly. It is now designed to fly. It has new desires and abilities.

The butterfly is no longer a worm and should not be called a worm. It is no longer something ugly but has been made into something beautiful. We never call a butterfly a converted worm; yet some Christians make the mistake of saying, "I'm just a sinner saved by grace." The believer is rarely called a sinner in Scripture, but a saint, a new creation, compete in Christ!

The old man we inherited from Adam is dead; the new man that we now are, we inherited from Christ. One was sinful, and is now dead. The other is righteous and is now alive,

> *God made Him who had no sin to be sin for us, so that in Him we might become the righteousness of God* (2 Corinthians 5:21).

Our true identity is that of righteous saints, not sinners.

We can only have one basic identity. If we had two, and old one and a new one, we would be both a child of God (1 John 3:1) and a child of Satan (John 8:44). We would be both *in Christ* and *in Adam*. We were physically born *in Adam*. At our new birth, we were transferred from being *in Adam* to being *in Christ*. This is sometimes called *the exchanged life*.

Our deepest basic identity cannot be both sinful and righteous.

Our body and soul can, at various times, act righteous, or act sinful. But our spirit, the deepest essence of who we are, cannot be both righteous and sinful. It is either made in the likeness of Adam (sinful), or in the likeness of Christ (righteous). It cannot be both.

We must understand the difference between our identity and our experience. We are always a perfect 10 in our identity, but in practice we may be a 4 or a 5. But until we understand our identity and apply it, we will never have a consistent Christian experience.

The Scriptures teach that a believer's spirit exists in union with the Lord's Spirit,

> *But the one who joins himself to the Lord is one spirit with Him* (1 Cor. 6:17).

Christ has permanently united Himself to our spirit. Would God have done so if our spirit, the essence of our being, was sinful? Scripture answers that question,

> *For what do righteousness and wickedness have in common? Or what fellowship can light have with darkness?* (2 Corinthians 6:14).

If our spirit were sinful, God would not join Himself to it. But God can join Himself to our spirit because He has recreated it in the likeness of His righteousness.

I used to watch my mother can food in glass jars. First, she would sterilize them so they would not contaminate the food she put in them. She had to cleanse them before she could fill them. We were cleansed by Christ's death on the cross so He might fill us with His Spirit.

Scripture describes the believer's warfare from the perspective of the believer's single identity, not a split identity. We are not schizophrenic with two natures, wondering who we are. We should not think we are Dr. Jekyll one day and Mr. Hyde the next. We can no longer use our identity to justify sin because we no longer have an old nature.

The Christian does not have an old nature and a new nature; he has a new nature and what the Apostle Paul calls the flesh; which is controlled by indwelling sin. The battle is not between the old nature and the new nature but rather betweem the flesh and the Spirit,

> *For the flesh desires what is contrary to the Spirit, and the Spirit what is contrary to the flesh. They are in conflict with each other, so that you do not do what you want* (Galatians 5:17).

(Unfortunately some translations translate *flesh* as *old nature*. But they usually have a footnote signifying that the Greek word means *flesh*.)

The believer does engage in spiritual warfare. But the enemy is not some part of the believer's essential being. Rather, it is the believer's flesh and its power of sin in his members that the believer is to reign over. Our warfare is not us against ourselves. It is us and the Holy Spirit who are aligned against the flesh (or power of sin) that inhabits our earthly bodies.

When we truly understand who we are in Christ we will want to live consistent with our true identity. We are a hypocrite when we sin because we are not acting consistent with who we are in Christ.

Understanding our true spiritual identity will have a profound effect in our life as is demonstrated in the following letter I received from an inmate.

> *Greetings in Christ Jesus our precious Lord. I wanted to write you with all my heart thanking the Lord and thanking you for allowing the Lord to use you in writing* The Grace Discipleship Course. *You have no idea, through your teaching and the Word of God, how much my life has changed.*
>
> *In fact, it's now 2:30 a.m. I'm locked up in a 8 X 12 cell for the night but I'm in tears of joy, truly rejoicing for my eyes to have been open to the truth of who I am in Christ and what He's done for me that I could never do for myself.*
>
> *After over thirty drug rehabs, several mental institutions, sixteen times in jail and prison four times, I'm finally free!*
>
> *I'm thirty-seven years old and I've been addicted to drugs since I was twelve and to crack cocaine since I was seventeen.*
>
> *I accepted Christ at the age of twenty-one but I lived a life of defeat all these years because I tried to do my best to please God and when I failed I usually ended up right back into drugs and bondage.*
>
> *I would get out of jail and whole heartedly go to church and try to do right but it was only temporary. I obtained plenty of Bible knowledge while incarcerated but knowledge didn't work either. It wasn't until I had to lose everything, friends, family and coming back to*

jail that I came to the point where I had no where to look but to God and I cried out with everything I had for Him to take my life. I prayed, "Please Lord either take my life right now, or do such a miracle in me that when I walk out from these showers (I had ran to the only place in jail where I could be alone to cry out in the shower) I will be a walking miracle." He answered my prayer like I would have never imagined.

I maintained contact with him after he was released and rejoiced that he had an effective ministry; a demonstration of the miracle that God had worked in his life.

Chapter 2

IN CHRIST WE HAVE
THE QUALITY OF HIS LIFE

Identity is a powerful force. The word *identity* comes from the Latin idem, meaning, the same. Webster says it is,

> *The state or fact of being identical; sameness, as distinguished from similitude and diversity.*

Fans wear their team's colors and cheer. When their team wins, they say, "We won?" even though they just sat and watched. They feel a oneness with their team and are impacted by its performance. They are thrilled when their team wins and depressed when they lose. That's the power of identity.

The Apostle Paul wants us to know our identity in Christ. When Christ won, we won, even though we just sat and watched through reading or hearing the Word. Once we know our sameness in Christ, it will change our life. We will say,

> *But thanks be to God, who always leads us in triumphal procession in Christ* (2 Corinthians 2:14).

Like fans that cheer and tear down the goal posts, we can joyously follow in His *triumphal procession* and daily participate in His victory.

In the Roman triumphal processions, the victorious general rode his white war horse up the Via Sacra to the temple of Jupiter on the Capitoline Hill. This procession went through the Roman forum, the center of trade and government buildings, and consisted of Roman army with flags flying, captured prisoners, and wagons full of plundered treasures.

On a trip to Rome, I left our travel group at the Coliseum and went across the street to get a closer look at Titus' Arch of Triumph, which was built in commemoration of General Titus' sacking of Jerusalem in 70 A.D. I had heard that there was a relief (a sculptured picture) featuring the Jewish captives. A fence prohibited me from getting close to the Arch, but with my telephoto lens I was able to take a picture of a relief inside the Arch that pictured the Jewish people carrying the Menorah, the sacred candelabrum with seven branches used in the Temple in Jerusalem. Chills went up and down my spine as I was impacted by the physical evidence of this historical event.

At Jesus' first coming, He rode in humiliation on a colt. But at His second coming, He will come as the conqueror on His white war horse, coming to destroy the wicked and take control of the earth,

> I saw heaven standing open and there before me was a white horse, whose rider is called Faithful and True. With justice He judges and makes war...The armies of Heaven were following Him, riding on white horses and dressed in fine linen, white and clean (Revelation 19:11,14).

When Jesus returns the second time, believers will come with Him, as in a victorious march, on white horses to watch this epic event.

On the cross, He defeated all the forces of evil and later He will come to judge. Meanwhile, Paul knew that his readers would realize the meaning of the phrase, *triumphal procession in Christ*. In Christ, we follow in His triumphal procession. God's grace, that is unleashed in our lives, can produce a victorious life that is only available through Christ—who is our life,

> *But thanks be to God! He gives us the victory through our Lord Jesus Christ* (2 Corinthians 2:14)

He conquered sin for us. He doesn't ask us to do what He has already done. He only asks that we enter into His victory. Victory comes by letting Christ do what our struggling and striving have failed to do.

Many believers don't realize that Jesus Himself has come to produce an abundant life that most can only dream about living. He will supply a never failing supply of power that will exceed even our fondest expectations.

Jesus came to live His life *in* us, yet most Christians try to live their life *for* Him.

A truck was in a collision and the driver was trapped. Six men lifted on the bumper trying to free him. Their veins stood out as they strained, but it was an impossible task. Finally a wrecker drove up but the only available spot was the bumper where the men were tugging. The driver of the wrecker said, "If you men will get out of the way, I will lift the truck off of the driver." As long as the men remained in the way, the wrecker could not be used. Many Christians let self get in the way of the Lord working in their lives. If we want Christ to live His life through us, we must get out of the way and let Him take control of our lives.

An unknown Christians said,

The most extraordinary thing about the victorious life is that although it is so clearly taught in Scripture, yet it is so frequently unrecognized by Bible students. Many who have a thorough knowledge of the Bible know nothing of this truth experientially. The writer himself had been a careful student of the Scripture for many years before the glory of this life lighted up his soul. Again and again clergy have confessed, 'We do not preach this truth because we do not know it experientially.'

—*How to Live the Victorious Life*, p. 105

Miles J. Stanford notes that many great saints labored for years before understanding and experiencing this truth,

We might consider some familiar names of believers whom God obviously brought to maturity and used for His glory—such as Pierson, Chapman, Tauler, Moody, Goforth, Mueller, Taylor, Watt, Trumbull, Meyer, Murray, Havergal, Guyon, Mabie, Gordon, Hyde, Mantle, McCheyne, McCorkey, Deck, Paxson, Stoney, Saphir, Carmichael, and Hopkins. The average for these was 15 years after they entered their life work before they began to know the Lord Jesus as their Life and ceased trying to work for Him and began allowing Him to be their all in all and do His work through them.

—*The Green Letters*, pp. 7-18.

Francis Schaeffer, a man who probably influenced Christianity more than anyone during the 20th century, ministered for more than ten years before he understood the power of the resurrected Christ in his life.

He recognized that his own lack of reality of the presence of God in his life was related to his ignorance about the meaning of the finished work of Christ in his present life,

> *Following his revival experience, he asked Edith* (his wife) *a question he has asked others over and over again, 'Edith, I wonder what would happen to most churches and Christian work if we awakened tomorrow, and everything concerning the reality and work of the Holy Spirit, and everything concerning prayer, were removed from the Bible. I don't mean just ignored, but actually cut out—disappeared. I wonder how much difference it would make?' ... There is no source of power for God's people—for preaching or teaching or anything else—except Christ Himself. Apart from Christ, anything which seems to be spiritual power is actually the power of the flesh."*
> — *Francis Schaeffer The Man and His Message,*
> pp. 71-73,75.

What is this source of power? Jesus said,

> *I am come that you might have life and have it to the full* [or abundantly] (John 10:10).

This life is not an extension of our life, but the very life of Christ. He not only imparts to us the duration of His life, which is eternal, but also the quality of His life—His love, joy, peace, etc. The life He gives is full and abundant because it is His life with all His qualities.

We are told,

For if, by the trespass of the one man, death reigned through one man, how much more will those who receive God's abundant provision of grace and of the gift of righteousness reign in life through the one man, Jesus Christ (Romans 5:17).

How much more and *abundant* are from the Latin, *ab* and *undare*, it means *to rise in waves,* never ending.

Sit by the seashore and watch one wave after another dash on shore as far as the eyes can see. The love of Christ is deeper that any ocean and can continuously flood in to meet your every need.

The Greek word, *abundance,* can mean a mathematical number greater than another; something left over. A woman looked at the Sahara desert and said, "I'm glad to see, for once, something there's enough of."

But everything in the world has a limit, except God's grace. There is always a surplus of God's grace,

Now to Him who is able to do immeasurably more than all we ask or imagine, according to His power that is at work within us.

Paul uses adjectives like wave after wave supplying inexhaustible grace.

Spanish coins before 1492 showed the strait of Gibraltar with the inscription, *Ne Plus Ultra,* meaning, *No More Beyond.* After Columbus, the inscription was changed to, *Plus Ultra,* meaning, *More Beyond.* There is always more beyond of God's grace.

God did not just kill off our *old man* and leave us to live the Christian life by our own resources,

His divine power has given us everything we need for life and godliness" (2 Peter 1:3).

The next verse says this is possible because we may *participate in the divine nature...* (v. 4).

When we were born again spiritually we not only received the life of Christ, but we also received the quality of His life. Because of our identity with Christ, what happened to Christ, happened to us. When He died, we died. When He was buried, we were buried. When He arose, we arose. When He ascended, we ascended. He is seated in a place of victory and we are there with Him, *And God raised us up with Christ and seated us with Him,* it happened to us. We could refer to it as our co-death, co-burial, co-resurrection, and co-ascension with Christ. Don't quickly pass over this verse but take time to ponder it; it is fact, truth, and reality.

Facts are to be reckoned as true, even if we don't feel like it. For example, you get up and look at the sun and say, "The sun rose this morning." But we know that the sun didn't rise, rather the earth rotated into the plane of the sun's light. We have learned to accept this as a fact, even though our feelings indicate otherwise. So ponder the truth of your identity with Christ until it impacts your soul.

We sing *there is power in the blood,* but where are the songs about the *power of His resurrection?* I get goose bumps when I sing, *I will cling to the old rugged cross.* However, the cross was an instrument of death. Would we sing, "I will cling to my old magnum 357?" The cross killed off the *old man,* paid sin's penalty, cleansed us, and reconciled us to God. It made us dead to the law and dead to the world, but it didn't give us His life. We no longer cling to the cross, but He clings to us because He is in us.

31

Christians wear crosses, but where are the symbols of the empty tomb? We have songs about the cross; but where are the songs about the power of His resurrection? There absence eloquently condemns contemporary Christianity's ignorance of the great truth that Christ is our life. In his book *The Christ Life for the Self Life*, F. B. Meyer said,

> *I never can understand why the Church has made so little of the resurrection and ascension.*

Some writers say that our *counting*, or *reckoning*, ourselves dead keeps the *old man* on the cross. But Scripture says that he is dead. Our co-death, burial, and resurrection are fact, truth, reality, whether we believe it or not.

As a former sailor, I was taught how to use *dead reckoning* to navigate from one position to another. You must calculate your current position by using a previously determined position, or fix, and advancing that position based upon known or estimated speeds over elapsed time and course. However, *dead reckoning* is subject to cumulative errors because of using estimates of speed and direction that have many variables. However, there are no variables in God's Word!

> *In the town hall in Copenhagen stands the world's most complicated clock. It took forty years to build at a cost of more than a million dollars. That clock has ten faces, fifteen thousand parts, and is accurate to two-fifths of a second every three hundred years. The clock computes the time of day, the days of the week, the months and years, and the movements of the planets for twenty-five hundred years. Some parts of*

that clock will not move until twenty-five centuries have passed.

What is intriguing about that clock is that it is not accurate. It loses two-fifths of a second every three hundred years. Like all clocks, the timepiece in Copenhagen must be regulated by a more precise clock, the universe itself. That mighty astronomical clock with its billions of moving parts, from atoms to stars, rolls on century after century with movements so reliable that all time on earth can be measured against it.

— Haddon Robinson in *Focal Point*.

There are no variables in God's Word,

For no matter how many promises God has made, they are 'Yes' in Christ (2 Corinthians1:20).

We can trust it when it describes our identity in Christ. However, do we really believe it and apply it to our lives?

Music can be real, but our ears must hear it before it becomes real in our experience. A beautiful sunset is real, but we will not enjoy it if we don't open our eyes and experience it. Paul said,

I pray also that the eyes of your heart may be enlightened in order that you may know the hope to which He has called you, the riches of His glorious inheritance in the saints (Ephesians 1:18).

We will not enjoy the riches we have in Christ until we appropriate them by faith.

Our experience is entering into Christ's history—His experience in time. The effects of our co-death, burial, and resurrection become real in our experience when we accept the facts into our life by faith.

Watchman Nee shares his insights on reckoning,

For years after my conversion I had been taught to reckon. I reckoned from 1920 to 1927. The more I reckoned that I was dead to sin, the more alive I clearly was. I simply could not believe myself dead and I could not produce death. Whenever I sought help from others I was told to read Romans 6:11, and the more I read Romans 6:11 and tried to reckon, the further away death was; I could not get at it. I fully appreciated the teaching that I must reckon, but I could not make out why nothing resulted from it. I have to confess that for months I was troubled. I said to the Lord, 'If this is not clear, if I cannot be brought to see this which is so very fundamental, I will cease to do anything. I will not preach anymore; I will not go out to serve Thee anymore; I want first of all to get thoroughly clear here.' For months I was seeking, and at times I fasted, but nothing came through.

I remember one morning—that morning was a real morning and one I can never forget—I was upstairs sitting at my desk reading the Word and praying, and I said, 'Lord, open my eyes!' And then, in a flash, I saw it, I saw my oneness with Christ. I saw that I was in Him and that when He died I died. I saw that the question of my death was a matter of the past and not of the future, and that I was just as truly dead as He was because I was in Him when he died. The whole thing had dawned upon me. I was carried away with such joy at this great discovery that I jumped from my chair and cried, 'Praise the Lord, I am dead!' I ran downstairs and met one of the brothers helping in the

kitchen and laid hold of him. 'Brother,' I said, 'do you not know that Christ had died? Do you not know that I died with Him? Do you not know that my death is no less truly a fact than His?' Oh, it was so real to me! I longed to go through the streets of Shanghai shouting the news of my discovery. From that day to this I have never for one moment doubted the finality of that word: 'I have been crucified with Christ.'
— *The Normal Christian Life*, pp. 58-59.

Some unsaved people try to live a life they don't have and some Christians *don't live the life they do have!*

If you don't have His life, trust in Christ's finished work on the cross and receive it. If you are a believer, have you *counted* or *reckoned* your oneness with Christ in His death, burial, and resurrection and experienced the quality of His life? You will not be a victorious Christian until you do.

In his book *Forever Triumphant*, F. J. Huegel told a story that came out of World War II. After General Jonathan Wainwright was captured by the Japanese, he was held prisoner in a Manchurian concentration camp. Cruelly treated, he became "a broken, crushed, hopeless, starving man."

Finally, the Japanese surrendered and the war ended. A United States army colonel was sent to the camp to announce personally to the general that Japan had been defeated and that he was free and in command. After Wainwright heard the news, he returned to his quarters and was confronted by some guards who began to mistreat him as they had done in the past. Wainwright, however, with the news of the allied victory still fresh in his mind, declared with authority, "No, I am in command here! These are my orders." Huegel observed that from that moment on, General Wainwright was in control.

Huegel made this application:

Have you been informed of the victory of your Savior in the greatest conflict of the ages? ... Then rise up to assert your rights. ... Never again go under when the enemy comes to oppress. Claim the victory in Jesus Name. We must learn to stand on resurrection ground, reckoning dead the old creation life over which Satan has power, and living in the new creation over which Satan has no power whatever.

Chapter 3

IN CHRIST WE CAN LIVE BY THE SPIRIT

We can experience the quality of Christ's life by living by the Spirit. Paul writes,

> *So I say, live by the Spirit and you will not gratify the desires of the flesh* (Galatians 5:16).

Four times this is mentioned in this chapter: *live by the Spirit* (verse 16 and 25); *led by the Spirit* (verse 18); *live by the Spirit*, and *keep in step with the Spirit* (verse 25). Learn to do this and sin will not control your life.

Live by or *walk in* refers figuratively to our way of life. It is in the present tense, meaning that we are to keep on being controlled by the Spirit. After a one time surrender to Him, it should then become a *continuous attitude*. Paul wrote,

> *So then, just as you received Christ Jesus as Lord, continue to live in Him rooted and built up in Him, strengthened in the faith as you were taught, and overflowing with faithfulness* (Colossians 2:6).

How did we receive the Lord? By faith trusting Him as our savior. How do we *live in Him*? By faith trusting in Him and His power and not in the flesh.

The Lord Jesus gave us the supreme example of what it means to walk in the Spirit. Although He was God, yet as man all His activities, every step He took and every word He said and every decision He made He did so as man. Jesus was man in perfection — totally, unquestioningly available and that is why all power was available to Him. As man in perfection He had an unlimited call upon the inexhaustible supplies of deity.

The inexhaustible supplies of God are available to the man who is available to all the inexhaustible supplies of God. We will never be deity, but the inexhaustible supplies of deity are available to us as we *walk (live) in the Spirit.*

> *His divine power has given us everything we need for life and godliness* (2 Peter 1:3).

Many Christians work hard at trying not to sin. They are like a person who keeps pulling weeds out of his yard. He can rip off the heads, but they grow back. He can say to the Lord, "Help me pull weeds!" The Lord says, "I love you too much to teach you to pull weeds. I'm going to teach you how to grow healthy grass, it will crowd out the weeds." We concentrate on the wrong thing—sin. God says,

> *Walk (live) in the Spirit and you will not gratify the desires of the flesh* (Galatians 5:16).

Some believers keep repenting of besetting sins, but can never clear the weeds out on their own. The Lord says, *live by the Spirit and you will not gratify the desires of the flesh.* If we have a trust relationship with Him, He will crowd out the weeds by growing grass. *Growing in grace* is like *growing in grass*. Concentrate on Him and you won't be preoccupied with the weeds.

Those who practice *performance religion* are preoccupied with keeping our lawn looking nice so others will say, "How nice!" But they never grow in grace.

Christ's power in us will keep us from sin,

> *in order than the righteousness requirement of the law might be fully met in us, who do not live according to the flesh but according to the Spirit* (Romans 8:4).

The key is to have our minds set on Him,

> *Those who live according to the flesh have their minds set on what the flesh desires: but those who live in accordance with the Spirit have their minds set on what the Spirit desires* (verse 5).

What the *flesh desires* is outlined in Galatians 5:19-21, and they are labeled as *acts of the flesh* that are all sinful because that is all the flesh can produce.

In contrast, the *fruit of the Spirit* are listed in verses 22-23 and they are all supernatural. Verse 23 ends with, *against such there is no law.* They mark a supernatural life that only Christ can live in us through the Holy Spirit.

Paul instructed us,

> *Rather, clothe yourselves with the Lord Jesus Christ, and do not think about how to gratify the desires of the flesh* (Romans 13:14).

The word *gratify* means to *fulfill, to bring to an end.* It is used 8 times in Revelation to bring things to completion.

James explains how gratifying the desires of the flesh causes us to sin,

> *When tempted, no one should say, 'God is tempting me.' For God cannot be tempted by evil, nor does He tempt anyone; but each one is tempted when by his own evil desire, he is dragged away and enticed. Then, after desire has conceived, it gives birth to sin, and sin, when it is full grown, gives birth to death* (James 1:13-15).

In the garden, Adam and Eve first looked, then lusted, and then finally sinned. There is nothing new; there is always the world, the flesh, and the Devil that will entice us to sin. We can't help but look, sin is all around us, but we can stop lust at the door of our mind. Paul assured us that,

> *No temptation has seized you except what is common to man. And God is faithful, He will not let you be tempted beyond what you can bear. But when you are tempted, He will also provide a way out so that you can stand up under it* (1 Corinthians 10:13).

Curiosity is what got Adam and Eve in trouble. A teacher was winding down a discussion in a fourth-grade class on the importance of curiosity. "Where," she asked, "would we be today if no one had ever been curious?" One hand shot up, "In the Garden of Eden."

Sometimes when we are tempted, we need to be like Joseph; when he was tempted by Potaphar's wife he just ran. If we sin it is our fault because we did not immediately take the *way to escape* that God provided.

The conflict rages between the flesh and the Spirit,

For the flesh desires what is contrary to the Spirit, and the Spirit what is contrary to the flesh. They are in conflict with each other, so that you do not do what you want (Galatians 5:17).

The word *flesh* is used in different ways; here it does not refer to the physical body, but rather the sin principle in us that Satan uses as a beachhead to entice us to sin. Unbelievers are said to be *in the flesh — when we were in the flesh* [not saved] (Romans 7:5). This is the condition of a person who does not belong to Christ.

In contrast, the Christian is described,

You, however, are controlled not by the flesh but by the Spirit, if the Spirit of God lives in you. And if anyone does not have the Spirit of Christ, he does not belong to Christ (Romans 8:9).

Notice that in this one verse, *the Spirit of God* and *the Spirit of Christ* are used interchangeably. It is proper to say that *the Holy Spirit lives in us*, and also that *Christ lives in us*.

The believer is no longer *in the flesh*, but he can *live after the flesh*. Living after the flesh describes a believer that lives by his own resources and is, subsequently, controlled by sin. The saint can live after the flesh, but he is always in the Spirit.

Paul defines believers as being *spiritual* and *worldly* (King James Version *carnal* or *fleshly*),

And I, brethren, could not speak unto you as unto spiritual, but unto carnal, even as unto babes in Christ (1 Corinthians 3:1).

Fleshly Christians are living as though they were separated from Christ, their source of power.

Spiritual Christians are those who,

live by the Spirit, and you will not gratify the desires of the flesh (Galatians 5:16).

One definition of sin could be *satisfying a legitimate need in an illegitimate way*. God placed every need we have in us and will provide a legitimate way to meet those needs.

Dirt in the garden is good; dirt on the living room rug is bad. Sex outside of marriage is bad, sex in marriage is good. Satisfying our hunger is good, but gluttony is bad. There is a spiritual way and a fleshly way to meet these God given needs.

Paul says,

For the flesh desires what is contrary to the Spirit (Galatians 5:17).

The word *contrary* is a compound Greek work *antikeinai, anti—against,* and *keimai—to lie.* New Testament passages refer to our flesh as our adversary, it is at war with the Spirit and sometimes causes us to do things that we don't want to.

The Christian life is not just passive where we *let go* and *let God* do it. There is always an act of the will. Paul said,

No, I beat my body and make it my slave so that after I have preached to others, I myself will not be disqualified for the prize (1 Corinthians 9:27).

He was not talking about losing his salvation, but rather of being put on a shelf as far as his usefulness for God was concerned.

The surrender of our wills to God does not crush into fatalistic abandon the very faculties that God endowed us with. On the contrary, the surrendered saint immediately finds his faculties marvelously quickened; his mind, emotions, and will. All the powers of his soul-life are renewed. God now

> works in you to will and to act according to His good purpose (Philippians 2:13).

The key is,

> live by the Spirit, and you will not gratify the desires of the flesh (Galatians 5:16).

But our will is involved, we have a choice. A defeated Christian may say, "But I have tried!" That's the problem; we can't, but He can. We must quit trying and start trusting to release His power in our lives. The Holy Spirit is infinitely ready, but He is a gentleman, He leads but never compels. This is a mystery, but also a fact that God is working in us to reveal His will; but on the other hand, we must choose to follow His will. Both truths are taught in Scripture.

Galatians chapter 5 contrasts the *works of the flesh* (verse 19), with the *fruit of the Spirit* (verse 22). Who controls our life, the flesh or the Spirit? Our life will bear witness by producing either *works of the flesh* or *fruit of the Spirit*.

When we react to something, the flesh usually kicks in first then the Spirit has to put the brakes on our actions. If a car pulls out in front of you, the flesh will say, "Ram him, he shouldn't have done that!" But then the Spirit quickly convicts us by saying, "Hold it, Saints don't act that way."

Conversely, when the Spirit moves the flesh will resist. That is why we are to pray because, *the spirit is willing but the flesh is weak* (Matthew 26:41). We are also told that we are *weak through the flesh* (Romans 8:3). But we are reassured,

> *You, dear children, are from God and have overcome them, because the One who is in you is greater than the one who is in the world* (1 John 4:4).

When we sin, we can't *cop a plea* and say *the devil made me do it*, it is our responsibility.

> *Real, physical pressure is a lot like the pressure of temptation. You can 'escape' it only to a point. Do you think a submarine, since it's airtight, can go down as deep as it likes? It cannot. Even the nuclear submarines built strongly enough to batter through the ice at the North Pole have a maximum depth. A submarine known as Thresher exceeded that depth some years ago. When the pressure became too great, the seawater crushed the sub's heavy steel bulkheads as if they were a plastic model. Searchers found only little pieces of that huge submarine. The tremendous weight of the sea had smashed its strong steel hull. That is pressure!*
>
> *Yet there are fish which live at the same depth in which the Thresher was crushed. How can these fish survive so deep? The answer is that they have equal pressure within themselves. For us, temptation is much the same as the tremendous pressure of the sea. We can only survive only with Christ in us.*

-Philip Yancy, Tim Stafford,
Unhappy Secrets of the Christians Life, p. 25.

There is a spiritual war going on, but we don't need to be crushed by the pressure because,

> *You, dear children, are from God and have overcome them, because the One who is in you is greater than the one who is in the world* (1 Peter 4:4).

Like the fish, we are able to survive under pressure. When outside pressures threaten to crush us, the Holy Spirit dwelling in us, is able to offset it with inward pressure that will enable us to bear up under it.

Scripture says,

> *For we know that our old self was crucified with Him so that the body of sin might be done away with (rendered powerless), so we should no longer be slaves to sin"* (Romans 6:6,7).

We are to

> *count yourselves dead to sin but alive to God in Christ Jesus, Therefore do not let sin reign in your mortal body so that you obey its evil desires* (verses 11-12).

Our responsibility is to *offer the parts of our body as the instruments of righteousness* (verse 13), and *to obey Him as slaves* (verse 16).

There are no spectators in this spiritual war. God has equipped us to be victorious,

His divine power has given us everything we need for life and godliness through our knowledge of Him (2 Peter 1:3).

He dwells in us so we can *participate in the divine nature and escape the corruption in the world caused by evil desires* (verse 4).

The great evangelist Dwight L. Moody testified,

When I was converted, I made this mistake; I thought the battle was already mine, the victory already won. But I found out after serving Christ for a few months that conversion was only like enlisting in the army, that there was a battle on hand.
—D. L. Moody, *Two Worlds*, April 3, 1978, p. 10.

The key to victory is to be *led by the Spirit, you are not under law* (Galatians 5:18). The contrast is between the Spirit and the Law. Which one governs us?

Led by the Spirit is like a young boy being led by a slave until he is adopted as an adult son and then must take responsibility for his actions. Paul says,

For when we were controlled by the flesh, the sinful passions aroused by the law were at work in our bodies, so that we bore fruit for death. But now, by dying to what once bound us, we have been released from the law so that we serve in the new way of the Spirit, and not in the old way of the written code (Romans 7:5-6).

We are either controlled by the Spirit or the law, we can't be controlled by both. The problem comes when Christians try to mix them it produces guilt, not power and joy.

The Law speaks to the flesh and produces dead works and sin. Grace speaks to the spirit and produces fruit of the Spirit. When we put ourselves under the law it produces guilt vs. total forgiveness; weakness of the flesh vs. the power of the Spirit; fear vs. love.

The law only entices us to sin,

> But sin, seizing the opportunity afforded by the commandment produced in me every kind of covetous desire. For apart from law, sin is dead (Romans 7:8).

A father joined a professional diet group. His family was delighted and felt that now he would be able to get his weight under control. However, when he came home from his first session with the group, he headed straight for the refrigerator. "What happened?" gasped his wife. He replied, "I'm starving, all they did was talk about food!"

The law only stirs up sin. Put a man in a dusty room with a broom and tell him to sweep it up and he will begin to cough. Dust is like sin and the broom is like the law, all it does is make a mess, create dust, and moves it around. If someone comes in with the gospel of grace, it is like a vacuum cleaner which will suck up the dust and you don't need the broom of the law.

Someone suggested that if you want to know when a person is ready to be released from a mental hospital, just put him into a room with a mop. Turn on a water faucet and let the water run out on the floor. If he starts to try to mop it up, he is not ready to be released. However, if he goes over and turns off the facet he is sane enough to make it on the outside.

No believer has a big enough broom or mop to clean up his life, only surrendering to the Spirit's control can vacuum up the sin in our life.

Many believers are saved by faith but kept by struggle; exhausting themselves trying to live the Christian life.

Harry Houdini made a name for himself by escaping from every imaginable confinement — from straightjackets to multiple pairs of handcuffs clamped to his arms. He boasted that no jail cell could hold him. Time and again, he would be locked in a cell only to reappear minutes later.

It worked every time — but one. He accepted another invitation to demonstrate his skill. He entered the cell, wearing his street clothes, and the jail cell door shut. Once alone, he pulled a thin but strong piece of metal from his belt and began working the lock. But something was wrong. No matter how hard Houdini worked, he couldn't unlock the lock. For two hours he applied skill and experience to the lock but failed time and time again. Two hours later, he gave up in frustration.

The problem? The cell had never been locked. Houdini worked himself to near exhaustion trying to achieve what could be accomplished by simply pushing the door open. The only place the door was locked was in his mind.

Jesus unlocked the door and set the prisoners free. The door is open, don't be a frustrated prisoner of your own making, walk out by faith and enjoy a victorious life of *living in the Spirit.*

Chapter 4

IN CHRIST WE ARE
SEATED WITH HIM IN HEAVEN

Paul challenged believers to claim their glorious inheritance in the saints,

> *I pray also that the eyes of your heart* (or understanding) *may be enlightened in order that you may know the hope to which He has called you, the riches of His glorious inheritance in the saints, and His incomparably great power for us who believe. That power is like the working of His mighty strength* (Ephesians 1:18,19).

He wanted their head knowledge to become heart knowledge so they could experience *His incomparable great power*. Then he gave two illustrations of God's power: Illustration number one,

> *...which He exerted in Christ when He raised Him from the dead and seated Him at His right and in the heavenly realms, far above all rule and authority, power and dominion, and every title than can be given, not only in the present age but also in the one to come* (Ephesians 1:20,21).

This power was so great that it raised Christ's dead body from the grave and seated Him in the place of power in heavenly realms. Christ now has all authority over all rulers and authorities throughout eternity.

Illustration number two:

> ...made us alive with Christ even when we were dead in transgressions—it is by grace you have been saved. And God raised us up with Christ and seated us with Him in the heavenly realms in Christ Jesus (Ephesians 2:5,6).

What happened to Christ happened to us because we were in Him. The supernatural power that raised Christ from the grave and seated Him in heavenly realms did the same to us spiritually.

There are three things Paul says happened to us:

1. A resurrection: God *made us alive together with Christ*. This refers to our receiving the very life of Christ.
2. An ascension: *raised up with Christ* and,
3. An enthronement, *and seated us with Him in the heavenly realms in Christ Jesus.*

Those are not merely theological phrases. They represent realities which have already happened and we desperately need to understand these great truths.

Notice, all the verbs are in the past tense. This is something which has happened, not something which is going to happen. It has already occurred when you believed in Jesus Christ. You don't have to work toward it. It is not something which great saints achieve after years of effort. It is something which is already true, and happened to every believer.

If we attended a funeral and viewed a corpse that we knew was utterly dead and had lost all ability to live in any sense whatsoever. If we had the power to lay hands on him so that he came to life again here and now, it would be heralded all the over town. And yet that is exactly what the apostle says occurs in the inner spiritual life of a man when he passes from death to life when he believes in Christ. We are no longer dead after we believed. We have been made alive with Christ, raised with Christ, and seated with Christ in Heaven.

Some commentators say that believers are not yet in Heaven, but only have spiritual blessings from Heaven. But Robertson's New Testament Word Pictures says in Ephesians 2:6 the believer is conceived as already seated with Christ.

These same truths were also taught by Paul in Romans chapter six about our co-death, burial, resurrection, and ascension with Christ. The believer's spirit is now glorified and seated in heavenly places with Christ. We dwell below in our 'earth suit' to do His will, but our identity is with Christ in *heavenly realms*. Because of our identity in Him, what happened to Him happened to us.

If you put a piece of paper in a book, it is inseparably identified with that book. If you bury it in the ground, it would be in the ground. If you put it into a NASA exploration to Mars, it would be on Mars. Because we are baptized into Christ's death, burial, resurrection, and ascension we are inseparable from Him.

How many messages have you heard on the believer's ascension with Christ? Not many, if any at all. That is why believers are so defeated. We are seated with Christ in a place of victory. Write it in red capital letters in your life, I

> *have been raised with Christ ... where Christ is seated at the right hand of God* (Colossians 3:1,2).

We are not to struggle to have victory; we face earth's struggles from a place of victory. We can say,

> *But thanks be to God, who always leads us in triumphal procession in Christ* (2 Corinthians 2:14).

Many believers probably quickly pass over this statement that says we are now spiritually seated with Christ in heaven, thinking "This is too good to be true!" But that's why the gospel is called the *good news!* The cross not only punched our ticket to Heaven; we can experience the power of His resurrection now. Don't play it down! God did it! He *raised us up with Christ Jesus* (Ephesians 2:5,6). This is such a wonderful truth that Paul calls it,

> *The glorious riches of this mystery, which is Christ in you, the hope of glory* (Colossians 1:27).

Some Christians would blush if they said, *I am seated in heavenly places with Christ.* But to deny the reality of God's Word is calling God a liar. If you are seated in a building, you can deny the reality of it and say, "No, I'm outside of it." You can even picture yourself pounding on the door to get in; but that won't change reality, you are inside! Your location is based on fact, not feelings.

Many Christians live defeated lives because they don't understand their identity in Christ. The mild mannered Clark Kent, in the time of crisis, would enter a phone booth and emerge as a victorious muscled hero. We are asked to step into the 'phone booth' of our identity with Christ to have the *eyes of our heart* enlightened in order that we may experience *His incomparably great power for us who believe* (Ephesians 1:18-,19).

Paul repeats this great truth in Colossians,

> *Since, then, you have been raised up with Christ, set your hearts on things above, where Christ is seated at the right hand of God. Set your minds on things above, not on earthly things. For you died and your life is now hidden with Christ in God, when Christ, Who is your life appears, then you also will appear with Him in Glory* (3:1-4).

Notice that the past tense is used throughout these verses.

How can this be? We can accept the fact that Christ is in us through the Holy Spirit, but how can I be in Him? Paul writes,

> *But he who unites himself with the Lord is one with Him in Spirit* (1 Corinthians 6:17).

In Christ, we are now one with Him in spirit; when He comes, we will be with Him in our glorified body,

> *But we know that when He appears, we shall be like Him, for we shall see Him as He is* (1 John 3:2).

At that time our Savior will claim His trophy, the church,

> *His intent was that now, through the church, the manifold wisdom of God should be made known to*

> *the rulers and authorities in the heavenly realms* (Ephesians 3:10).

At the present time, heaven is where the real battle is fought,

> *For our struggle is not against flesh and blood, but against the rulers, against the authorities, against the power of this dark world and against the spiritual forces of evil in the heavenly realms* (Ephesians 6:12).

We battle against the unseen forces of evil.

How far away is heaven? There are dimensions that we do not see. When Elisha and his servant saw that the city was surrounded by an army with horses and chariots he said,

> *'Don't be afraid,' the prophet answered. 'Those who are with us are more than those who are with them.' And Elisha prayed, 'O Lord, open his eyes so he may see.' Then the Lord opened the servant's eyes, and he looked and saw the hills full of horses and chariots of fire all around Elisha* (2 Kings 6:16,17).

There are spiritual entities all around us that we cannot see,

> *Are not all angels ministering spirits sent to serve those who will inherit salvation?* (Hebrews 1:14).

Paul said that angels behold our worship,

For this reason, and because of the angels, the woman ought to have a sign of authority on her head (1 Corinthians 11:10).

It is difficult for us to conceive of something outside the dimensions of our world. In physics, three dimensions of space and one of time is the accepted norm. Even secular scholars accept the possibility of other dimensions. They propose many theories that require more dimensions; Superstring theory, M-theory, and Bosonic string theory that suggest the possibility of 10, 11, and 24 dimensions.

Imagine that you are inside of a big TV set (old tube type) that consisted of your world and someone touched the screen with one finger; all you could see was that small sample of what was outside. If they put their whole hand on the screen you would still be limited to what you had seen. You could not conceive that there were millions of other created people and animals outside your little box inhabiting the earth and a vast universe beyond. You would be limited to what was revealed to you. Likewise, we are limited to what God has revealed to us.

God has revealed many things to us about our relationship to heaven:

Our names are written there. We are to ...*rejoice that your names are written in heaven* (Luke 10:20);

Our citizenship is in Heaven. *But our citizenship is in Heaven. And we eagerly await a Savior from there, the Lord Jesus Christ* (Philippians 3:20).

Paul was writing to the city of Philippi which was a Roman colony that had many Roman citizens in it. Because of their loyalty, they were rewarded with the title *colonia*. From then on all who were free born became Romans citizens with the same privileges as those born in Rome. They were Roman citizens in Philippi.

Paul addressed them by saying, *To the saints in Christ Jesus, at Philippi* (Philippians 1:1). They were *in Christ* but physically at Philippi. To the Ephesians saints he said, *To the saints in Ephesus the faithful in Christ Jesus* (Ephesians 1:1).

Peter wrote, *Dear friends, I urge you, as aliens and strangers in the world...* (1 Peter 2:11). Aliens were considered *foreigners* (Greek word *para*, alongside, and *oikeo*, to make one's home. Resident aliens were permitted to reside without rights as citizens and could be expelled without right of appeal. It would be like not having a birth certificate or passport.

We are aliens on this planet earth physically while spiritually seated in heavenly places. We are aliens here and our capital is New Jerusalem.

> *But you have come to Mount Zion, to the heavenly Jerusalem, the city of the living God. You have come to thousands upon thousands of angels in joyful assembly, to the church of the firstborn, whose names are written in heaven* (Hebrews 12:22-23).

The writer to the Hebrews spoke of Abraham,

> *By faith he made his home in the promised land like a stranger on a foreign country; he lived in tents* (temporary), *...For he was looking forward to the city with foundations, whose architect and builder is God* (Hebrews 11:9-10).

Ur of the Chaldees, that Abraham left, was a city of great splendor. Royal Tombs contained immense amounts of luxury items made of precious metals and precious stones. The buildings had great foundations. It was a city of temples and towers called ziggurats, all within a great wall overlooking the waters of the Euphrates. But most of it today lies crushed by the debris of succeeding civilizations and layers of fertile silt left by Noah's Flood. Abraham's faith was correct; Ur lies in rubble while believers, just like Abraham, look for that city that has foundations—the New Jerusalem.

Believers were commended for their faith,

> *And they admitted that they were aliens and strangers on earth. People who say such things show that they are looking for a country of their own. ... Instead, they were longing for a better country—a heavenly one. Therefore God is not ashamed to be called their God, for He has prepared a city for them* (Hebrews 11:13, 14, 16).

Our inheritance is in Heaven.

> *...An inheritance that can never perish, spoil or fade—kept in heaven for you* (1 Peter 1:4).

All of earth's monuments, awards, and treasures will be destroyed—only what's done for Christ will last. A young man attended our church one time who wore a tee shirt that read on the front, "The guy with the most toys," and on the back it read, "Still dies!"

That is why we are admonished,

> *Do not store up for yourselves treasures on earth, where moth and rust destroy, and where thieves break in and steal. But store up for yourselves treasures in Heaven...For where your treasure is, there your heart will be also* (Matthew 6:19,20).

We should have the attitude of the songwriter who wrote:

This world is not my home I'm just passing through
My treasures are laid up somewhere beyond the blue
The angels beckon me from Heaven's open door
And I can't feel at home in this world anymore.

Our savior is in Heaven.

...while we wait for the blessed hope—the glorious appearing of our great God and Savior, Jesus Christ (Titus 2:13).

We are His ambassadors on earth.

We are, therefore, Christ's Ambassadors, as though God were making His appeal through us. We implore you on Christ's behalf: Be reconciled to God (2 Corinthians 5:20).

Christians need to understand their job description before they can perform their job well. Teachers teach, runners run, and artists create art, but what do ambassadors do?

Ambassadors are diplomats of the highest rank, formally representing the head of state, with full authority to represent the government. Jesus said,

All authority in heaven and on earth has been given to me. Therefore go and make disciples of all nations (Matthew 28:18,19).

We have His authority to be ambassadors to all nations.

In other words, an ambassador stands in the place of the ones he represents, since the people cannot represent themselves. When meetings occur with foreign nations, it is the ambassador who has been chosen as the single person with the authority to speak for his country.

An ambassador is in a foreign land. His life is spent among a people who usually speak a different language, have different traditions, and a different way of life. Christians live in world that they are not to be conformed to because they are citizens of Heaven. We are strangers in an alien world.

An ambassador speaks for his own country, it is his government's message, decisions, and polices he conveys. We do not create our own message, but the message from our King; Jesus said, *and teaching them to obey everything I have commanded you* (Matthew 28:20).

The honor of a country is in its ambassador's hands. His country is judged by him. His words are listened to; his deeds are watched. The honor of Christ is in our hands and is to be upheld by our every word and deed.

Our affections are to be on heaven,

> *Since, then, you have been raised with Christ, set your hearts on things above, where Christ is seated at the right hand of God. Set your minds on things above, not on earthly things. For you died, and your life is now hidden with Christ in God. When Christ who is your life appears, then you also will appear with Him in glory* (Colossians 3:1-4).

The Arctic Tern has the longest migratory tour of any bird, 24,000 miles over trackless oceans. After it is hatched and old enough to feed itself, the parents leave. Weeks pass and finally the young Terns also leave for a place they have never seen or known. The Tern's parents could not have given them instructions; they didn't leave a note saying fly south until you see the Southern Cross, then go S by SW. God had built deep within them a longing for home.

God placed within every believer a longing for home. We are aliens and strangers who are subconsciously drawn toward Heaven.

Our affections are not to be of the world,

> Love not the world or anything in the world. If anyone loves the world the love of the Father is not in them. For everything in the world—the lust of the flesh, the lust of the eyes and the pride of the life is not of the Father but is of the world" (1 John 2:15,16).

If we understand and experience our life in Christ we can say with the Apostle Paul,

> May I never boast except in the Cross of our Lord Jesus Christ, through which the world has been crucified to me, and I to the world (Galatians 6:14).

Dr. Donald Grey Barnhouse relates the time he realized he was seated with Christ in the heavenlies,

> How well I remember the day I first went through to heaven. I was on shipboard crossing the Atlantic and had been reading and rereading Ephesians. Lying back in the deck chair, eyes closed, poring over its meaning, suddenly I saw the great truth of our ascension with Christ. My heart leaped as I saw the new and living way from myself to the throne of God where the Lord Jesus Christ desired me to join him by faith. It was like looking at a castle through a long lane of trees. Fortunately I was almost

alone on that part of the deck. I lifted my New Testament as though it were a sword (which it really is), and with the great Ephesian truth aflame before me, I shouted inwardly, 'Lord, I'm coming through!' Suddenly, it seemed as though I were in the heavens far above, looking down on a ship, a tiny dot on a blue sea. Although I was one of the specks on that ship, I know that henceforth, that ship, that ocean, and that world would be forever unimportant because I was in the heavenlies, joined by faith to my Lord. He was nearer than when I had seen Him at the cross. The eternal life which He gave me I now recognized as the life of eternity, which I was privileged to live in time while seated in the heavenlies with Christ."

Chapter 5

IN CHRIST WE ARE
ADULT SONS

The believer has this wonderful promise,

For you did not receive a spirit that makes you a slave again to fear, but you received the Spirit of sonship. And by Him we cry, Abba, Father (Romans 8:15).

The believer is now adopted into God's family as an adult son. He is now indwelled by Christ through the Holy Spirit. He is no longer under law, but under the supervision of a more effective master than the external law of the Old Covenant.

The word *adoption* and *adult son* had great meaning to Paul's Roman audience. The word *adoption* actually means *a son-placing*, and has nothing to do with taking an orphaned child and making him a member of a family. The Romans acknowledged all children as part of the family, but only those who went through the ritual of *son-placing* were recognized as sons. A Roman father, if he had male children, never referred to them as his sons until they were of age—they were his children, but they were not his sons.

But when the child became of age (about 14 to 17), the father took him down to the public forum where the child was publicly adopted by his own father, and thereafter regarded as an adult son in the family, being heir of the father and sharing privileges as well as the responsibilities.

Until he was son-placed, a child was like a slave legally and could only act through a legal representative. In the Greek and Roman culture, a child was under the supervision of a guardian (Greek word *paidagogos* — *a child-discipler* or *child-leader.*)

The *paidagogos* was not, in our sense of the word, a teacher at all. His duty was to accompany the boy to school each day and to see to his conduct in the street. He was to train the child in morals, manners, and deportment. His aid was to improve the soul, and train it up to live a virtuous, not an intellectual life.

Paul made an application of this custom,

> *Before this faith came, we were held prisoners by the law locked up until faith should be revealed. So the law was put in charge to lead us to Christ that we might be justified by faith. Now that faith has come, we are no longer under the supervision of the law* (Galatians 3:23-25).

When Paul spoke of the law bringing us to Christ, he meant the law was inadequate and would be replaced by something greater. The believer has been freed from being a slave to the law and placed under a higher supervision— the indwelling Holy Spirit,

> *What I am saying is that as long as the heir is a child, he is no different from a slave, although he owns the whole estate. He is subject to guardians and trustees until the time set by his father. So also, when we were children, we were in slavery under the basic principles of the world* (Galatians 4:1-3).

Under the New Covenant, the believer is no longer a slave to the law, but is adopted into the family as an adult son with all rights, honors, and responsibilities.

Historians write,

The one who is adopted becomes the legitimate and necessary heir of the one who adopts him. This quality of heir, much deeper among the Greeks than among the Romans or in modern legislation, implied the most complete continuation of the Person of the deceased; thus the adopted one acquired as elements of his inheritance, not only the property but also the name of the deceased, all his rights of relationship, his dignities and honors as well, succeeded to his judgments and debts. Upon the adopted one fell the responsibility for all minor children subsequently born to the one who adopted him.

—From Daremberg and Saglio *Dictionnaire Des Antiquites*; which was an authority on the ancient world.

Scripture states,

In love He predestined us to be adopted as His sons through Jesus Christ, in accordance with His pleasure and will (Ephesians 1:5).

As sons, believers have:

- *every spiritual blessing in Christ;* (Ephesians 1:3);
- *redemption* (v. 7);
- are *seated with Him in heavenly places* (Ephesians 2:6);
- *made joint-heirs,* (Romans 8:17); and
- *will reign with Him* (Revelation 20:6).

In the Jewish culture, on a boy's 13th birthday, the father will take the boy to the synagogue on the next Sabbath to celebrate his Bar Mitzvah. He is then a *Son of the Law*. Previously, the law had been administered through the father. Now the son is responsible for obedience to the law.

At the Bar Mitzvah, the father utters this benediction:

> *Blessed be thou oh God who hath taken from me the responsibility of this boy.*

The boy prayed this prayer:

> *Oh my God, and God of my father. On this solemn and sacred day, which marks my passage from boyhood to manhood, I humbly raise my eyes unto Thee and declare with sincerity and truth that henceforth I will keep Thy commandments and undertake to bear the responsibility of my actions toward Thee.*

In becoming an adult son, the believer is no longer to be led by the externals of the law, but is now under the direct supervision of the indwelling Holy Spirit,

> *Because you are sons, God sent the Spirit of His Son into our hearts, the Spirit who calls out, 'Abba, Father.' So you are no longer a slave, but a son; and since you are a son, God has made you an heir* (Galatians 4:6).

> *In first-century Palestine, a little Jewish child between 14 and 18 months of age would say 'Abab-ab-Abba,' the Aramaic equivalent of 'daddy'. No devout Jew would ever dream of addressing Jehovah, the high and lofty One, with such a childlike familiarity. It would*

seem disrespectful. Yet Jesus taught His disciples to pray, 'Our Father'. German scholar Gerhard Kittel pointed out that though the gospel writers used the Greek term for father, Jesus probably used the Aramaic Abba in all cases, particularly when He addressed God. This intimate father-child relationship to God was something wholly new to Judaism.

—D.J.D. *Our Daily Bread.*

Under Roman law, children between ages 14 and 17 (the age was not fixed), would turn in his robe, *Toga Protexta*, which means *Preparation*, for the, *Toga Verilas* in a ceremony called, *Liberalia*. They were liberated from their *pedagogos*, or guardian, who led them by the hand to the market and disciplined them. They were now adopted as an adult son. This ceremony took place in the Roman forum. The girl would take all her dolls, the boy his toys and offer these *childish things* as a sacrifice to Apollo. From that time on they were to act responsibly as adult sons and daughters.

In *The Robe* by Lloyd Douglas, Lucia described the ceremony of her older brother.

Father had bought Demetrius, (the Corinthian slave), six years ago and presented him to Marcellus on his seventeenth birthday. What a wonderful day that was, with all their good friends assembled in the Forum to see Marcellus, clean shaven for the first time in his life, step forward to receive his white toga. Cornelius Capito and father had made speeches, and then they had put the white toga on Marcellus. Lucia had been so proud and happy that her heart had pounded and her throat had hurt. She was only nine then and couldn't know much about the ceremony except that Marcellus was expected to act like a man now...."

Later, Marcellus tells a friend about the ceremony, "When a Roman of our sort comes of age, Paulus, there is an impressive ceremony by which we are inducted into manhood. Doubtless, you felt as I did, that this was one of the high moments of life. Well, do I remember the thrill of it! It abides with me still. How our relatives and friends assembled that day in the stately Forum Julium. My father made an address, welcoming me into Roman citizenship. It was as if I had never lived until that hour. I was so deeply stirred, Paulus, that my eyes swam with tears. And then good old Cornelius Capito made a speech, a very serious one, about Rome's right to my loyalty, my courage, and my strength. I know that old Capito had a right to talk of such matters and I was proud that he was there. They beckoned to me, and I stepped forward. Capito and my father put the white toga on me and life had begun.

Do you remember when your *eyes swam with tears* as Christ placed the *white toga* of His righteousness on you and welcomed you into His family as an adult son?

Do we realize the exalted position and privileges that were bestowed on us? He unlocked the handcuffs of the law that bound us in guilt and powerlessness. We are no longer restricted to the impersonal, external guidance of the law with its letters in stone; He put His law into our hearts and gave us over to the inward, personal supervision of the Holy Spirit.

As an adult son, the Holy Spirit gives us the power to live up to our responsibilities,

Therefore, there is now no condemnation for those who are in Christ Jesus, because through Christ Jesus the law of the Spirit of life set me free from the law of sin and death.....in order that the righteous requirement of the law might be fully met in us, who do not live according to the flesh but according to the Spirit (Romans 8:1-4).

We now have an intimate relationship with God and can call him, *Abba, Father.* During the Cuban missile crisis, President John F. Kennedy and his leaders, day after day, were burning the midnight oil trying to resolve the problem. A unique picture appeared on the front pages of many newspapers. It showed the president, the most powerful person in the world, standing behind his desk surrounded by Henry Kissinger and other distinguished cabinet members. The grim faces of the men standing behind the desk reflected the gravity of the situation. However, under the desk, was the President's son, John, playing with his toys.

White House security would not allow any other boy access so he joyfully played under the president's desk during such a crisis.

Scripture states,

For by Him all things were created: things in heaven and on earth, visible and invisible, whether thrones or power or rulers or authorities; all things were created by Him and for Him (Colossians 1:16).

To such a God we are invited as sons to come into His presence and call Him, "Abba (Papa) Father."

Chapter 6

IN CHRIST WE ARE JOINT HEIRS

This story was reported by Channel 5 in Kansas City, Missouri,

> An as yet unnamed Kansas City woman has become the recipient of the largest payout of unclaimed funds in Missouri (and maybe in US) history. A check was issued to her in the amount of $6.1 million dollars. It represented a single investment security which, unknown to the woman, had grown in value over the years into a veritable fortune.
>
> While we aren't disclosing this person's name, what I can tell you is we found this person and worked quickly to get the money back in her hands," said State Treasurer Clint Zweifel. "Assets become Unclaimed Property every day for many reasons, whether it is a death in the family, misplaced documents or a change in address. What is important though is Missourians know we will safeguard their money forever until they claim it, and they can search 24 hours a day.
>
> Over the past few years, the state of Missouri has returned approximately $103 million to more than 303,000 recipients who searched for and found their unclaimed property.

As joint heirs with Christ, we have a much greater inheritance than the woman in Missouri. And God has promised us to safeguard our inheritance,

an inheritance that can never perish, spoil or fade —
kept in Heaven for you (1 Peter 1:4).

We are not dependent on man's promises like an old man who had trouble communicating with his family so he got a new hearing aid. A week after he started using it, he went back to the specialist for a routine follow up. The specialist asked, "How is the hearing aid working?" The old man replied, "Great!" The specialists asked what his family thought about it. The old man replied, "Oh, I haven't told them yet—but I've changed my will three times."

The Apostle Paul states,

Now if we are children, then we are heirs — heirs of
God and co-heirs with Christ in order than we may
also share in His glory (Romans 8:17).

There is a difference between being an adult son as we mentioned in the last chapter and a co-heir. For instance, the term 'first-born' normally means the oldest son. He enjoyed perogatives over his brothers, like receiving the father's blessing (Genesis 27:1-4), preferential treatment by the father (43:33), respect as leader among the brothers (37:22), and a double portion of the inheritance (Deuteronomy 21:17).

Another example would be if two brothers inherited an estate as equal heirs, then the estate would be divided into two equal parts and each would be given the same amount. But the Christian is in spiritual union with Christ because of the new birth and is, therefore, a joint heir to the entire inheritance.

We have, *received the Spirit of sonship. And by Him we cry, 'Abba, Father*. God is our Father, therefore, we are heirs who will inherit our Father's property.

But God has another Son, one who is the first-born of every creature and heir of all things,

> *but in these last days He has spoken to us by His Son, whom He appointed heir of all things, and by whom He made the universe* (Hebrews 1:2).

Therefore, we are *joint heirs with Christ*. Like links in a chain that connects these truths together. The *spirit of sonship* (adoption) proves the fact of adoption; and by that adoption we are now adult sons; and if children, then heirs; if heirs, heirs of God. But there is another heir, therefore, we must be joint heirs with Christ.

For a will to be in effect it must be legal. The same Spirit of sonship that causes us to cry *Abba Father*, also guarantees our inheritance,

> *And you were also included in Christ when you heard the word of truth, the gospel of your salvation. Having believed, you were marked in Him with a seal, the promised Holy Spirit, who is a deposit guaranteeing our inheritance* (Ephesians 1:13-14).

Our inheritance is secure. Paul says,

> *For you died, and your life is now hidden with Christ in God* (Colossians 3:3).

One preacher was trying to drive home the fact that the believer was secure in Christ. He put a coin in his left hand and closed his fist over it saying, "That coin represents me and how I am *hidden with Christ.*" Then he closed his right hand over his left hand and said, "That represents me being *hidden with Christ in God,* and in addition to that I'm sealed by the Holy Spirit." Then he exclaimed, "For Satan to get at me he'd have to bust the Godhead!"

There is no flaw in God's will in regards to Christ. There is no probate court that could declare it invalid, *Who will bring any charge against those whom God has chosen?* (Romans 8:33). There is immutability in God's promise.

We signed the legal papers to adopt one of our sons in a judge's chambers. He pointed to a picture of his large family and mentioned that several of them were adopted. Then he told us that according to the law of our state we could never disinherit our adopted children. If that is true of man's laws, God says we are infinitely more secure when we are sealed by the Holy Spirit.

Joint heirs do not have rights individually that can be separated from the other heirs. One cannot sell or possess any part of the estate apart from the other. He has no rights unless it is agreed by the other. Christ, as co-heir, has identified Himself with us and our rights cannot be separated from Him. Even if we wanted to sell, He wouldn't because He has promised, *an inheritance that can never perish, spoil or fade—kept in Heaven for you* (1 Peter 1:4).

As sons of God, we are joint heirs of all that Christ possesses, and His possessions are infinite. Therefore, our possessions as believers are infinite.

To have an association with a great man is a distinguished mark of honor; to be co-heir with some great person would project great status. But no honor compares with being a joint heir with the King of kings, the Wonderful Counselor, the Mighty God, the Everlasting Father, The Prince of Peace!

The believer, being in Christ, has no superior on earth; there is no more dignified relationship than those who are joint heirs with Christ. There are many consequences of being a joint heir.

As joint heirs, we are also joint-sufferers.

> *Now if we are children, then we are heirs—heirs of God and co-heirs with Christ, if indeed we share in His sufferings in order that we may also share in His glory* (Romans 8:17).

Because of our identity with Christ, we share everything with Him—including suffering, *For we were all baptized by one Spirit into one body* (1 Corinthians 12:13). Paul describes the spiritual body of Christ in terms of the physical body. He says that there is one body but many members: hands, feet, etc. Then in verse 26 he explains,

> *so that there should be no division in the body, but that its parts should have equal concern for each other. If one part suffers, every part suffers with it; if one part is honored, every part rejoices with it.*

We can't change our oneness with our body. If our foot or hand gets an infection, the whole body can become feverish and shake. We can't change our oneness in the body of Christ,

> *If the world hates you, keep in mind that it hated me first. ... Remember the words I spoke to you: 'No servant is greater than his master.' If they persecuted me, they will persecute you also* (John 15:18,20).

During His earthly life, Jesus had no place to lay His head, was hated, persecuted, and finally crucified.

Paul stated,

> *For it has been granted to you on behalf of Christ not only to believe on Him, but also to suffer for Him* [or 'in His place'] (Philippians 1:29).

When Paul was converted on the Damascus road, Jesus said to him, *Saul, Saul, why do you persecute me?* (Acts. 9:4). Paul was persecuting the church which was the body of Christ.

Church #1 was the body of Christ incarnate on earth.
Church #2 is the spiritual body of Christ on earth today.

Later Paul said,

> *Now I rejoice in what was suffered for you, and I fill up in my flesh what is still lacking in regard to Christ's afflictions, for the sake of his body, which is the church* (Colossians 1:14).

Paul was saying that just as Christ suffered for the church, he was rejoicing that he could be a partaker of Christ's suffering.

Again Paul referred to Christ's sufferings,

> *For just as the sufferings of Christ flow over into our lives, so also through Christ our comfort overflows* (2 Corinthians 1:5).

But suffering will be rewarded,

Blessed is the man who perseveres under trial, because when he has stood the test, he will receive the crown of life that God has promised to those who love Him (James 1:12).

One man heard this verse and said, "Boy, am I blessed!"

We are identified with Christ as joint heirs which includes joint suffering and joint glory. Peter wrote,

Dear friends, do not be surprised at the painful trial you are suffering, as though something strange were happening to you. But rejoice that you participate in the sufferings of Christ, so that you may be overjoyed when His glory is revealed (1 Peter 4:12-13).

We might say, "But I don't want to suffer." Be patient, we are told,

For our light and momentary troubles are achieving for us an eternal glory that far outweighs them all (2 Corinthians 4:17).

Our *light and momentary troubles,* must be weighed against an *eternal glory* that defies description and lasts for all eternity. In perspective, our present life is only a speck in the ocean of eternity.

How long is eternity? If a bird could take a speck of earth and fly to deposit it on the moon on a trip that took a thousand years; then makes trip after trip until all the earth was deposited on the moon, eternity would not have yet begun. Eternity is infinite because time will be no more.

Paul said our troubles are *achieving for us an eternal glory that far outweighs them all.* What is this glory?

As joint heirs, Christ will share all things with us.

All things are yours, whether Paul or Apollos or Cephas or the world, or life or death or the present or the future—all are yours, and you are of Christ, and Christ is of God (1 Corinthians 3:21-22).

You can't get more comprehensive than that—all that God has is ours! Don't just pass over this verse, ponder it because it seems too good to be true, believers are joint heirs to everything God owns!

As joint heirs, Christ will share His glory. The word refers to the revelation of God in Christ, *He reflects the glory of God* (Hebrews 1:3). God's glory reflects all of His divine attributes such as His majestic holiness, etc. Jesus prayed,

And now, Father, glorify Me in Your presence with the glory I had with You before the world began (John 17:5).

As God, Jesus' glory was veiled in His fleshly body except on the Mount of Transfiguration when His glory was allowed to be briefly manifested.

As joint heirs, we are to glorify Christ.

All I have is yours, and all you have is mine. And glory has come to me through them (John 17:10).

Jesus gave this glory to believers, *I have given them the glory that you gave me* (John 17:22). It is humbling to think that glory can come back to Christ through believer's lives.

As joint heirs, Christ will share his glorified body with us.

But we know that when He appears, we shall be like Him, for we shall see Him as He is. Everyone who has this hope in Him purifies himself, just as He is pure (1 John 3:2-3).

We are to glorify him now in our bodies, but when He appears He will give us a glorified body like His own.

And just as we have borne the likeness of the earthly man, so shall we bear the likeness of the man from heaven (1 Corinthians 15:49).

If you don't like the way your body looks now, just wait; you will be satisfied with your new body, *I shall be satisfied when I awake in your likeness* [KJV] (Psalms 17:15).

As joint heirs Christ will share all He has with us.

...all are yours, and you are of Christ, and Christ is of God (1 Corinthians 3:22).

With NASA's space probes and the Hubble telescope, we are constantly discovering new facts and images of God's vast creation. Man is now discovering new marine life at a depth of seven miles in the Mariana Trench in the Pacific, which is the deepest part of any ocean.

Electron microscopes are able to achieve magnifications of up to about 10,000,000x, where ordinary light microscopes use magnifications below 2000x. A multitude of discoveries are revealing more about the complexity of God's smallest creations.

From the atoms too small to be seen, to the universe too vast to be fully explored, we own it all as joint-heirs in Christ!

As joint heirs, Christ will share His reign with us. We are told,

> *And God raised us up with Christ and seated us with Him in the Heavenly realms in Christ Jesus, in order that in the coming ages He might show the incomparable riches of His grace, expressed in His kindness to us in Christ Jesus* (Ephesians 2:6-7).

We are presently seated with Him spiritually, but will later reign with Him in our glorified bodies.

Notice the purpose clause in the above verse, *in order that.* The purpose is, *in the coming ages He might show the incomparable riches of His grace.* As we continue to consider *these incomparable riches,* they take our breath away. We cannot wrap our mind around such a promise of sharing His reign.

We are told that after the first resurrection,

> *Blessed and holy are those who have part in the first resurrection. The second death has no power over them, but they will be priests of God and of Christ and will reign with Him for a thousand years* (Revelation 20:6).

This will take place after we return with Christ when He comes from Heaven to judge and make war and set up His earthly kingdom,

> *I saw Heaven standing open and there before me was a white horse, whose rider is called Faithful and True.*

With justice He judges and makes war (Revelation 19:11).

Then in verse 14 it states that,

The armies of Heaven were following Him, riding on white horses and dressed in fine linen, white and clean.

These armies are the saints who return, not to help Jesus in the battle (they are unarmed), but to reign with Him after He defeats His enemies.

Reigning saints are not just some abstract spiritual exercise, but they will actually be governing over assigned responsibilities and even judge angels,

Do you not know that the saints will judge the world? ... Do you not know that we will judge angels? (1 Corinthians 6:2-3).

Enoch prophesied,

See, the Lord is coming with thousands upon thousands of His holy ones to judge everyone... (Jude 14-15).

As joint heirs, we will have a coronation day when we will be unveiled as the sons of God,

The creation waits in eager expectation for the sons of God to be revealed (Romans 8:19).

The *creation* includes everything in the physical universe except human beings whom He contrasts with in verses 22,23. Nature is sometimes personified in Scripture, *the desert and the parched land will be glad* (Isaiah 35:1).

The phrase, *eager expectation,* is a double compound Greek word that means, *to watch eagerly and with outstretched hand.* Like someone stretching way out to get a view of a touchdown; or jumping up and down to get a view over people.

The thought is repeated,

> *We know that the whole creation has been groaning as in the pains of childbirth right up to the present time* (Romans 8:22).

What are they eagerly awaiting for? *For the sons of God to be revealed* (verse 18). Because in that great day of our coronation,

> *...creation itself will be liberated from its bondage to decay and brought into the glorious freedom of the children of God* (verse 21).

Creation's *bondage to decay* started when Adam sinned,

> *Cursed is the ground because of you; through painful toil you will eat of it all the days of your life. It will produce thorns and thistles for you, and you will eat the plants of the field. By the sweat of your brow you will eat your food until you return to the ground* (Genesis 3:17-19).

Because of man's sin, God cursed the universe; and now, no part of creation entirely fulfills God's original purpose. If you ever fought crab grass you know that these words of Genesis can be taken literally.

Creation is in a state of corruption. The second law of thermodynamics is now in force which causes everything to degenerate and run down. Sin initiated the *law of the jungle* which caused nature, as the poet wrote, to be *Red in tooth and claw.*

Creation cannot rest until the plan of God is fulfilled. Until then, there will be natural disasters, wars, and unrest. History tells us that the birth pains of contractions are coming at increasing short intervals with more wars and unsolvable international conflicts.

The child of God also experiences these labor pains,

> *Not only so, but we ourselves, who have the first-fruits of the Spirit groan inwardly as we wait eagerly for our adoption as sons, the redemption of our bodies* (Romans 8:23).

We long to be liberated from these frail bodies that are subject to decay and death,

> *Now we know that if the earthly tent we live in is destroyed, we have a building from God, an eternal house in Heaven ... Meanwhile we groan, longing to be clothed with our heavenly dwelling* (2 Corinthians 5:1,2).

Paul reminds us,

> *But our citizenship is in Heaven. And we eagerly await a Savior from there, the Lord Jesus Christ, Who, by the power that enables Him to bring everything under His control, will transform our lowly bodies so they will be like His glorious body* (Philippians 3:20,21).

From the Fall of man, until now, all history has been marching toward the coronation day of believers, when Christ will display to Heaven and earth the result of His conquering grace as manifested in the church. Until then, believers groan along with all creation, eagerly anticipating that climactic day of our coronation as *sons of God*.

As joint heirs we will receive a new heaven and a new earth to go along with our new glorified body.

Not only has creation been affected by sin, but the whole universe has been contaminated and will have to be recreated. The *blessed hope* of the Christians will also affect all of creation. The final judgment will involve destruction of heaven and earth,

> *But the day of the Lord will come like a thief. The heavens will disappear with a roar; the elements will be destroyed by fire, and the earth and everything in it will be laid bare* (2 Peter 3:10).

There will be a *roar*, a *big bang*, a nuclear explosion, and the elements will be destroyed.

The *elements* are the atomic components into which matter is ultimately divisible, which make up the composition of all created matter. Peter means that the atoms, neutrons, protons, and electrons are all going to disintegrate. The earth in its present form along with the entire universe will be consumed.

Scoffers used to make fun of the unlearned fisherman, Peter, talking about elements being destroyed with a roar. However in 1947, at White Sands, New Mexico the first atomic bomb was detonated which vindicated God's word. Peter no doubt didn't understand what he was writing, but the Holy Spirit who inspired his writing did.

Our universe is a marvel of nuclear fusion. Billions of stars like our Sun are controlled nuclear explosions converting hydrogen into helium and providing light and heat.

But scientists are still trying to solve the puzzle of what holds matter together. They have built an 11 billion dollar accelerator in Bern, Switzerland to try to discover the *Biggs element,* or the *God particle,* that would help explain how creation came into being.

Scripture gives us the answer: Christ created and sustains the universe,

> *For by Him all things were created things in heaven and on earth, visible and invisible, whether thrones or powers or rulers or authorities; all things were created by Him and for Him. He is before all things, and in Him all things hold together* (Colossians 1:16-17).

By the power of His Word, He created all things and *in Him all things hold together.* At His Word, the *Divine nuclear glue* that holds matter together will be withdrawn resulting in the destruction of the heavens and the earth.

We are in one of two groups, those who will be glorified forever at His coming or punished for eternity,

> *This will happen when the Lord Jesus is revealed from heaven in blazing fire with His powerful angels. He will punish those who do not know God and do not obey the gospel of our Lord Jesus. They will be punished with everlasting destruction and shut out from the presence of the Lord and from the majesty of His power on the day He comes to be glorified in His holy people and to be marveled at among all those who have believed* (2 Thessalonians 1:7-10).

Notice that a person doesn't have to do anything to miss Heaven—just not obey the gospel and reject Christ as their savior.

If I am asked if I believe in the *Big Bang*, I say, "Yes, there is a big bang coming to your city—are you ready?" If not, you will face punishment at His *great white throne* of judgment,

> *Then I saw a great white throne and Him who was seated on it. Earth and sky fled from His presence, and there was no place for them. And I saw the dead, great and small, standing before the throne, and books were opened. Another book was opened, which is the book of life. The dead were judged according to what they had done as recorded in the books....If anyone's name was not found written in the book of life, he was thrown into the lake of fire* (Revelation 20:11,12,15).

The earth and sky fled from His presence, and there was no place for them, they will be replaced by a perfect new heaven, earth and universe free from sin. We marvel at our beautiful world around us, but we are looking at God's 'junk yard' that has been ruined by sin. Man's original sin brought death and destruction to mankind, the animal, and plant world.

The world-wide flood in Noah's time brought cataclysmic changes in the earth's structure. Deep seas were formed containing volcanoes and jagged deep trenches. Teutonic plates shifted by the flood pushed up mountains and plateaus. We marvel at their beauty and diversity, but we haven't seen anything yet. Just wait until we stand in silent amazement gazing at His new creation.

The new heaven and earth will contain vegetation and animals but we will marvel at a pristine creation untainted by sin. His new creation cannot be adequately described. The Apostle John used terms we are familiar with to try to explain Heaven; but we have never seen a street that was made of *pure gold, like transparent glass* (Revelation 21:21).

We stand in awe of God's wisdom and creativity to create the world we live in. Science continues to discover new complexity and diversity in the vast universe and microorganisms. We can only imagine what God's new creations will be!

You are a marvel of God's creation—you are God's Stradivarius.

Over the years there have been numerous theories and explanations offered up concerning the unique sound of a Stradivarius violin. Everything from climatic effects on the wood from the surrounding forests to secret molding techniques employed by the master craftsman. One of the more recent, scientifically based explanations is found in the illustration below.

> *Antonio Stradivarius was an Italian violin maker who lived from 1644-1737. His violins are now the most prized violins ever made because of the rich and resonating sound they produce. The unique sound of a Stradivarius violin cannot be duplicated.*
>
> *Surprisingly, these precious instruments were not made from treasured pieces of wood, but instead were carved from discarded lumber. Stradivarius, who was very poor and could not afford fine materials like his contemporaries, got [much] of his wood from the dirty harbors where he lived. He would take those waterlogged pieces of wood to his shop, clean them up, and from those pieces of trashed lumber, he would create instruments of rare beauty.*

It has since been discovered that while the wood floated in those dirty harbors, microbes went into the wood and ate out the center of those cells. This left just the fibrous infrastructure of the wood that created resonating chambers for the music. From wood that nobody wanted, Stradivarius produced violins that everybody wants.

Regardless of your past, if you are a believer, Christ dwells in you and can produce a life that will resonate with His glory.

There's a story of a great violinist who announced he would give a concert using an unusually expensive violin. On the designated night the hall was packed with violin lovers curious to hear such an instrument played. The violinist came out on stage and gave an exquisite performance. After bowing to thunderous applause, he suddenly threw the violin to the floor, stomped it to pieces, and walked offstage. The audience was horrified. The stage manager came out and said, "Ladies and gentlemen, to put you at ease, the violin that was just destroyed was only a twenty-dollar violin. The maestro will now return to play on the advertized instrument." He did so and few could tell the difference.

The point is obvious; it isn't primarily the violin that makes the music; it's the violinist. Most of us are twenty-dollar violins at best, but in the Master's hands we can make beautiful music.

Chapter 7

IN CHRIST WE ARE
FREE FROM THE LAW

In chapter 4 we saw that the believer is no longer a slave, but an adult son,

> *But when the fullness of time came, God sent forth His Son, born of a woman, born under the Law, so that He might redeem those who were under the Law, that we might receive the adoption as sons. Because you are sons, God sent the Spirit of His Son into our hearts, the Spirit who calls out, 'Abba, Father.' So you are no longer a slave, but a son; and God has made you also an heir* (Galatians 4:4-7).

Later in the chapter, Paul elaborates on this by giving an allegorical description of two sons:

> *Tell me, you who want to be under the law, are you not aware of what the law says? For it is written that Abraham had two sons, one by the slave woman and one by the free woman. His son by the slave woman was born in the ordinary way; but his son by the free woman was born as a result of a promise. These things may be taken figuratively, for the women represent two covenants. One covenant is from Mount Sinai and bears children who are to be slaves: This is Hagar.*

Now Hagar stands for Mount Sinai in Arabia and corresponds to the present city of Jerusalem, because she is in slavery with her children. But the Jerusalem that is above is free, and she is our mother (Galatians 4:21-26).

This is an allegory that teaches us deeper lessons of the riches we have in Christ.

There are:

1. Two Women—Hagar and Sarah
2. Two Sons—Ishmael and Isaac
3. Two Covenants—Law and Grace
4. Two Mountains—Sinai and Calvary
5. Two Cities—earthly Jerusalem and heavenly Jerusalem.

There are two mothers and sons that are contrasted; Hagar and Ishmael and Sarah and Isaac.

The mothers are described in a spiritual sense; Hagar a bondwoman and Sarah the free woman.

The sons were born, figuratively speaking; Ishmael born according to the flesh and Isaac born according to the promise or according to the Spirit.

The allegory is clearly contrasting the Old Covenant and the New Covenant.

Each proceeds from, figuratively speaking, a mountain and a city: Ishmael from Mt. Sinai, the present Jerusalem, and Isaac from Mt. Calvary, the Jerusalem above.

The spiritual status of the two offspring are: Ishmael is enslaved and Isaac is free.

The Abrahamic Promise

God had promised Abraham that his offspring would be as numerous as the stars in heaven and the sand on the seashores. However, Abraham was 86 and his wife Sarah was 76; too old to have children. After years went by Sarah had a great plan and took matters into her own hands. It was the custom in that day to have children by a concubine, so Sarah said to Abraham,

> *The Lord has kept me from having children. Go sleep with my maidservant* (Hagar); *perhaps I can build a family through her. Abram agreed to do what Sarah said* (Genesis 16:2,3).

The bondwoman bore a son in the ordinary way, and the freewoman's son through the promise is born of the Spirit. Fleshly scheming and faith are opposites and God required faith.

> *Abraham said, 'If only Ishmael might live under your blessing?' Then God said, 'Yes, but your wife Sarah will bear you a son, and you will call him Isaac. I will establish my covenant with him as an everlasting covenant for his descendants after him'* (Genesis 17:18,19).

God told Abraham that his fleshly scheme would not qualify to fulfill the promise, it required faith, not fleshly effort.

The flesh cannot attain the promise,

> *Jesus answered, 'I tell you the truth, no one can enter the kingdom of God unless he is born of water and*

the Spirit. Flesh gives birth to flesh, but the Spirit gives birth to spirit. You should not be surprised at my saying, 'You must be born again.' (John 3:5-7).

Ishmael was born of the flesh, and not by the supernatural promise of God, *his son by the slave woman was born in the ordinary way* (Galatians 4:23a).

The Jewish leaders thought that because they were Abraham's descendants *born in the ordinary way*, that they were OK spiritually,

> *They answered him, 'We are Abraham's descendants and have never been slaves of anyone. How can you say that we shall be free?' Jesus replied, 'I tell you the truth, everyone who sins is a slave to sin. Now a slave has no permanent place in the family, but a son belongs to it forever. So if the Son sets you free, you will be free indeed'* ... *'You belong to your father the devil and you want to carry out your father's desire'* (John 8:33-36, 44).

All Jews are natural descendants of Abraham, but are not his spiritual children unless they are born again spiritually.

Isaac was the son of the promise, *but his son was born as the result of a promise* (Galatians 4:23b). He was the result of a miracle because Abraham was 100 and Sarah was 90,

> *By faith Abraham, even though he was past age—and Sarah herself was barren—was enabled to become a father because he considered him faithful who had made the promise. And so from this one man, and he as good as dead, came descendants as numerous as the stars in the sky and as countless as the sand of the seashore* (Hebrews 11:11,12).

Ishmael was born of the flesh *in the ordinary way*, self effort; while Isaac was born of faith, *by the power of the Spirit* (Galatians 4:29).

Paul states,

> *If you belong to Christ, then you are Abraham's seed, and heirs according to the promise* (Galatians 3:29).

Believers are adult sons and joint heirs of the promise

> *Because you are sons, God sent the Spirit of His Son into our hearts, the Spirit who calls out, 'Abba, Father.' So you are no longer a slave, but a son; and God has made you also an heir* (Galatians 4:6,7).

There are several contrasts mentioned in this passage:

1. Two Covenants; The old Covenant, representing the law, and the new Covenant representing grace.
2. Two women had sons; Hagar, the slave woman, gave birth in the ordinary way, and Sarah, the free woman, gave birth as the result of a promise.
3. Two cities; Mount Sinai, the present city of Jerusalem that represents the law, and the Jerusalem that is above that represents grace.

The Two Women Represent Two Covenants

One covenant was represented by Hagar from Mount Sinai bearing children who were slaves; the other was Sarah bearing children representing the Jerusalem above which is free,

...for the women represent two covenants. One covenant is from Mount Sinai and bears children who are to be slaves; This is Hagar. Now Hagar stands for Mount Sinai in Arabia and corresponds to the present city of Jerusalem, because she is in slavery with her children. But the Jerusalem that is above is free, and she is our mother (Galatians 4:24-26).

Mount Sinai represents the present Jerusalem and the law, and the New Jerusalem from above that is free and represents grace.

Hagar was a bond servant, the property of her master and her children were the same. Her son, Ishmael, was born 14 years before Isaac, but that did not make him an heir. She represents Mount Sinai where God thundered forth the law. Hagar means *wanderer* or *fugitive*. Twice she fled to Arabia, which was outside the land which God promised to Abraham.

She was associated with the Arabs, her descendants populated Arabia. Both Jews and Arabs claim Abraham as their father and both claim the land. Conflict has been continuous since their birth to Abraham. The Arabs are not left out by God, but must come to Him by faith in Christ.

The *present city of Jerusalem* represents everyone who is in bondage to the law which produces spiritual slavery. This Jerusalem is dominated by salvation by works; the flesh trying to keep the law. Everyone who tries to be justified by the law is a slave to it.

Jerusalem was the center where the law was practiced in Paul's day and produced Judiasers who persecuted him.

The *Jerusalem that is above is free* and is *the mother* of everyone who trusts Christ. The present Jerusalem and the law represent an earthly system and speaks to an

to the sprinkled blood that speaks a better word than the blood of Abel (vv. 22-24).

In contrast to the gloom and doom of Mount Sinai, there is presented a *joyful assembly,* where those who have believed in Christ and were sprinkled by His blood have their *names written in heaven.* Their guilt has been replaced by joy because they are *righteous men made perfect.*

The law could never do what Christ accomplished on the cross,

> *Because by one sacrifice he has made perfect forever those who are being made holy* (Hebrews 10:24).

Believers are no longer children of the slave woman but sons of the free woman who look forward to the New Jerusalem,

> *'Come, I will show you the bride, the wife of the Lamb.' And he carried me away in the Spirit to a mountain great and high, and showed me the Holy City, Jerusalem, coming down out of heaven from God* (Revelation 21:10).

In Christ we are born free from the law

> *For it is written that Abraham had two sons, one by the slave woman and the other by the free woman. His son by the slave woman was born in the ordinary way but his son by the free woman was born as the result of a promise* (Galatians 4:22-23).

Believers are freed from the law because of their faith in Christ,

Clearly no one is justified before God by the law, because, 'The righteous will live by faith.' The law is not based on faith; on the contrary, 'The man who does these things will live by them.' Christ redeemed us from the curse of the law by becoming a curse for us ... He redeemed us in order that the blessing given to Abraham might come to the Gentiles through Christ Jesus, so that by faith we might receive the promise of the Spirit (Galatians 3:11-14).

Abraham was saved by faith before the law was given,

What I mean is this: The law introduced 430 years later, does not set aside the covenant previously established by God and thus do away with the promise. For if the inheritance depends on the law, then it no longer depends on a promise; but God in his grace gave it to Abraham through promise (Galatians 3:17,18).

The covenant made with Abraham was not based on his works; God put him into deep sleep and the covenant was made by God Himself. It was unconditional because it depended on God alone; man had nothing to do with it.

The law was given to show men their need of a savior

Before this faith came, we were held prisoners by the law (warden) locked up until faith should be revealed. So the law was put in charge to lead us to Christ that we might be justified by faith. Now that faith has come, we are no longer under the supervision of the law (Galatians 3:23-25).

Paul personified the law as a jailer of guilty, condemned sinners on death row awaiting God's judgment (Romans 6:23). Only faith in Christ unlocks the door of the prison and frees men bound by the law.

The law was to reveal man's utter sinfulness, his inability to save himself, and in desperate need of a Savior—it was never intended to be the way of salvation,

> *For when we were controlled by the flesh, the sinful passions aroused by the law were at work in our bodies, so that we bore fruit for death. But now, by dying to what once bound us, we have been released from the law so that we serve in the new way of the Spirit and not in the old way of the written code* (Romans 7:5,6).

Grace frees the believer from the law and legalism

> *For the law of the Spirit of life in Christ Jesus hath made me free from the law of sin and death* (Romans 8:2).

He declared the good news that the believer is no longer under law,

> *For sin shall not be your master, because you are not under law, but under grace* (Romans 6:14).

This does not mean the Christian is *lawless* and should not live a moral life. We are not lawless toward God, but inlawed to Christ as His bride. James speaks of the *perfect law that gives freedom* (James 1:25).

A widower with two small children hired a housekeeper as a servant. He told her what to cook, keep house, dress and care for the children. He checked up on her to see that she did it right and corrected her if she didn't. After two years, he married the woman and the relationship changed. He no longer followed her around to oversee her work. Nor does he tell her what to cook for dinner. She is his in a relationship of love and she delights to do his will. She asks him what he would like for dinner and goes to the trouble to prepare it. She is no longer under law—but grace.

We are inlawed to Christ as His bride and delight to do His will out of love. Paul states that *for Christ's love compels us* (2 Corinthians 5:14).

The believer is not lawless but is now indwelled with the Holy Spirit who exercises supervision over him,

> *in order that the righteousness requirement of the law might be fully met in us, who do not live according to the flesh but according to the Spirit* (Romans 8:4).

He lifts the believer to a higher plane and enables him to live a righteous life. An airplane can defy the law of gravity because its engines power allows a greater power to take over—the law of aerodynamics. Likewise, the believer is now given power that can overcome sin,

> *Because the One who is in you is greater than the one who is in the world* (1 John 4:4).

Christ now empowers believers to do something that the law could never do—live His righteous life through them.

The New Covenant believer has not only been cleansed from his sin because of the cross, he now has the resurrected life of Christ living in him to produce holiness.

Christ's death on the cross fulfilled the requirements of the law, and the Old Covenant, which was external.

Christ's resurrection life now allows us to live under the grace of the New Covenant which is internal.

Scofield contrasts law and grace,

> *Law curses; grace redeems from that curse. Law kills; grace makes alive. Law shuts every mouth before God; grace opens every mouth to praise Him. Law puts a great and guilty distance between man and God; grace makes a guilty man right to God. ... Law says, do and live; grace, believe and live. Law never had a missionary; grace is to be preached to every creature. Law utterly condemns the best man; grace freely justifies the worst. Law is a system of probation; grace, of favor. Law stones an adulteress; grace says, "Neither do I condemn thee; go, and sin no more." Under law the sheep dies for the shepherd; under grace the Shepherd dies for the sheep.*
>
> *Everywhere the Scriptures present law and grace in sharply contrasted spheres.*
>
> *The mingling of them in much of the current teaching of the day spoils both; for law is robbed of its terror, and grace of its freeness."*
>
> – C.I. Scofield, *Law and Grace, Rightly Dividing the Word of Truth*

Chuck Swindoll comments,

> *I can assure you, your old master doesn't want you to read this. He wants you to exist in the shack of ignorance, clothed in the rags of guilt and shame, and afraid of him and his whip. Like the cruel slave owner, he wants you to think you 'gotta take a beatin' every now 'n' then' just so you will stay in line. Listen to me today. That is heresy! Because our Savior has set*

us free, the old master—the supreme grace killer—has no right whatsoever to put a whip to your back. Those days have ended, my friend. You're free. Those of us who are a part of The Grace Awakening refuse to live like slaves. We've been emancipated!"

— The Grace Awakening, p. 109.

Chapter 8

IN CHRIST WE CAN
BE FRUITFUL

A scientist who believed in evolution told God, "I can make life out of dirt." God said, "Go ahead." The scientist replied, "Give me some dirt." God said, "Get your own dirt!"

There is an axiom (a self evident truth) that "Life can only come from life." Jesus said, *I am come that you might have life* (John 10:10). Christianity is the saving life of Christ. Religion can't produce it.

Jesus said,

> *I am the vine, you are the branches. If a man remains in Me and I in him, he will bear much fruit; apart from Me you can do nothing* (John 15:5).

We can't make spiritual life and we can't live the supernatural life. There is only one Man who ever lived that could live a supernatural life—the Lord Jesus Christ.

Under the Old Covenant, Israel was *the vine* and God the Father was the husbandman who tended the vine. However, after the death and resurrection of Christ, the New Covenant pictures Christ as the vine and believers as the branches,

I am the true vine, and my Father is the gardener (John 15:1).

Under the Old Covenant, the Father tilled but under the New Covenant, Christ gives life.

Many scriptures describe Christ as our life:

- *When Christ, who is your life* (Colossians 3:4);
- *For me to live is Christ* (Philippians 1:21);
- *We are partakers of the divine nature* (2 Peter 1:4).

Christ dwells in the believer through the Holy Spirit. *Abiding in Christ,* or *walking in the Spirit,* mean the same thing. Christ and the Holy Spirit are used interchangeably in the New Covenant scriptures,

> *...if the Spirit of God lives in you. And if anyone does not have the Spirit of Christ, he does not belong to Christ. But if Christ is in you...* (Romans 8:9,10).

Christ in us, the Holy Spirit in us, or *the Spirit of Christ in us,* are all referring to the same thing,

> *Christ in you the hope of glory* (Colossians 1:27).

The Holy Spirit is a person, not a force, quite different than *the force be with you* as in the Star Wars movie. The vine pictures the saving life of Christ living in us. Christianity is not a performance religion where we try to produce a supernatural life. The ornaments on a Christmas tree may dazzle us with their beauty, but they don't have life.

Two men were looking at the body of a young woman at a funeral. One said, "Isn't she beautiful." The other man replied, "Yes, she's beautiful—but dead!"

The secret of living is fruit bearing.

Why are we here? Charlie Brown told Lucy, "We are here to make people happy." Lucy replied, "What are all the other people here for?" Jesus tells us why we are here. Jesus mentions two types of branches,

> *He cuts off every branch in me that bears no fruit, while every branch that does bear fruit He prunes so that it will be even more fruitful* (John 15:2).

The dead branch He cuts off and the living branch He prunes.

The dead branch speaks of professors who are not possessors of Christ's life,

> *he is like a branch that is thrown away and withers; such branches are picked up, thrown into the fire and burned* (v. 6).

Believers have been made alive through faith in Christ,

> *Therefore, if anyone is in Christ, he is a new creation* (2 Corinthians 5:17).

Believers just need to be pruned so they will be more fruitful.

Fruit is produced by the inherent energy of a living organism and reveals the true character of the tree,

You shall know them by their fruit ... Even so every good tree brings forth good fruit, but a corrupt tree brings forth evil fruit" (Matthew 7:16,17).

Every living thing produces after its own kind. A person who is spiritually alive in Christ will show forth Christ's character. A dead person does dead things; a person outside of Christ cannot produce His supernatural life.

He prunes (corrects) the believer so he may produce more fruit. The Greek word *prunes* also means *cleans.* Jesus said,

Sanctify them by the truth Your Word is truth (John 17:17).

God's Word is like a wash cloth that wipes away sinful habits.

Why does a plant need to be pruned? Because they consume so much sap that there is none left to produce fruit. They grow unfruitful shoots called *suckers* that consume the sap that would otherwise produce fruit.

They are like believers who are sapped by the cares of the world and things that crowd out spiritual fruit. My sister-in-law has rose bushes that grow as tall as your head and are profuse with roses. I asked her how she did it and she replied, "I cut them back to stumps every year." Everything not needed for fruit bearing is ruthlessly cut back.

Jesus cursed a fig tree that didn't bear fruit and it withered and died. You might admire its healthy leaves but it was designed to bear figs, not leaves.

The believer is chastened that he might yield the fruit of righteousness,

Our fathers disciplined us for a little while as they thought best; but God disciplines us for our good, that we may share in his holiness. Now no chastening for the present seems to be joyous, but grievous; nevertheless afterward it yielded the peaceable fruit of righteousness unto them which are exercised thereby (Hebrews 12:10-11).

We can rejoice when God disciplines us because it proves that he loves us and is treating us as sons.

The secret of fruit bearing is abiding

Remain in me, and I will remain in you. No branch can bear fruit by itself; it must remain in the vine. Neither can you bear fruit unless you remain in me (John 15:4).

The word *remain* (King James Version *abide*) occurs three times in this one verse. The Greek word *remain* is used 12 times as *to remain beside*, and 8 times to be *in union*. For the sap to flow to the vine and produce fruit it must abide in the vine.

Union with Christ does not guarantee communion. When a man and woman form a marriage union, there is no guarantee that there will always be communion. If they do not communicate, they may not have a satisfying marriage.

When a person is born into the body of Christ, he is in an inseparable union with Him for eternity. He is bone of His bone and flesh of His flesh. However, we must constantly abide, communicate, and depend on Him if He is going to live His life through us and produce fruit,

...No branch can bear fruit by itself; it must remain in the vine. Neither can you bear fruit unless you remain in Me (John 15:4).

Our union with Christ is guaranteed, but communion is not. If we grieve the Holy Spirit, we can hinder His work in our lives,

And do not grieve the Holy Spirit of God with whom you were sealed for the day of redemption (Ephesians 4:30).

When we grieve Him we are still saved, but we cut off the flow of grace through our lives,

Let no corrupt communication proceed out your mouth but that which is for the use of edifying that it may minister grace to the hearer (Ephesians 4:29).

This verse precedes verse 30 that says *Do not grieve the Holy Spirit.*

When Christ is in control of our lives, we minister grace to others. However, we are warned,

See to it that no one misses the grace of God and that no bitter root grows up to cause trouble and defile many (Hebrews 12:15).

When we allow Christ to live through us, grace flows (v 29). When we *grieve the Holy Spirit*, (v 30), we no longer *minister grace to the hearer* (Hebrews 12:15).

Fruit produced by the Holy Spirit is different than *works* produced by human effort alone. In Galatians chapter 5 a distinction is made between *the acts of the flesh* (v 19) and the *Fruit of the Spirit* (v 22). Fruit of the Spirit is all good because it is supernatural; acts of the flesh are all bad.

A machine can perform work, but only life can bear fruit. Works can be done with the wrong motive, because of the law and fear. Only love can spontaneously bring forth Spiritual fruit.

Work implies effort; fruit is produced naturally and silently. It is the product of the inner life of Christ. If you walk through a vineyard you don't hear it growing, you only see the results of the growth. The law and legalism can produce zeal and good works without lasting spiritual results. It also wears down an individual and leads to exhaustion and burn out.

In contrast, fruit is produced by Christ working in us,

For it is God who works in you to will and to act according to His good purpose (Philippians 2:13).

It is a result of a *faith rest* in Christ as He works through us to *will* and to *act*. He changes our will so we are willing to do what He prompts us to do. Then He *acts* through us and gives us the power to accomplish His will.

Fruit results from the life giving sap from the vine. Jesus said, *...apart from Me you can do nothing"* (John 15:5). Jesus also said,

The Son can do nothing of Himself; He can do only what He sees His Father doing, because whatever the Father does the Son also does (v. 19).

How much could Jesus do without the Father?-- Nothing!

How much can we do without Jesus—Nothing!

Many Christians can be busy doing nothing. Jesus said, *the flesh counts for nothing* (John 6:63). We can spend a lifetime in the service of Jesus doing nothing!

As a born-again Christian, the life we possess is of Him, and it is to Him, and every moment we live here on earth must be through Him. Every activity we do on earth should be His activity in and through us; every step we take, every word we speak, everything we do, everything we are should be an expression of Christ in us working through us.

That is why Paul exhorts us to,

> *offer your bodies as living sacrifices, holy and pleasing to God — this is your spiritual act of worship* (Romans 12:1).

He also says,

> *offer the parts of your body to Him as instruments of righteousness* (Romans 6:13).

Jesus wants to think His thoughts through our minds, use our mouth to speak, and use our feet and hands to do His work.

There can be a one-time act of surrender, then a continuous attitude of obedience. Jesus supplies His grace moment by moment and not once for all. We can't manufacture His supernatural life anymore than we can raise a man from the dead. The branch is helpless without the vine. We only receive His power as we *abide* (walk or live) *in the Spirit*.

Ian Thomas said,

It is for you to be, it is for Him to do! Rest, fully available to the saving life of Christ.

Works of the flesh are usually initiated by man's will and then he asks God to bless his works. Man initiates, does the work, and gets the glory. The biblical formula should be: God initiates, we respond, God directs and empowers; God gets the glory, and we get the blessing.

We are cooperating with God like the helmsman of a sailboat. God tells us what direction to go, we steer the boat but the wind powers the boat to move. That is why it can be called a *faith rest*. God initiates, we respond, but He is directing and empowering, so it doesn't seem like work. In the end, God gets the glory and we are thrilled that God used us as co-laborers in His work. That doesn't mean that we never get tired, the great evangelist Dwight L. Moody once said,

I get weary in the work, but I never get tired of the work.

The secret of abiding is obeying

If you remain in Me and My words remain in you, ask whatever you wish, and it will be given to you. This is my Father's glory, that you bear much fruit, showing yourselves that you are My disciples (John 15:7,8).

My words remain in you means that we obey Him. If we really believe, we will obey. Jesus said,

Why call me Lord, Lord and do not do the things that I say? (Luke 6:46).

111

Paul said,

> *Know you not, that to whom you yield yourselves*
> *servants to obey, his servants you are to whom you*
> *obey; whether of sin unto death or obedience unto*
> *righteousness* (Romans 6:16).

No man is free; he can only choose which master he will obey.

We are saved for obedience,

> *Who have been chosen according to the foreknowledge*
> *of God the Father, through the sanctifying work of the*
> *Spirit, for obedience to Jesus Christ and sprinkling by*
> *His blood* (1 Peter 1:2).

The promise is that we will bear fruit if we obey,

> *If you remain in Me and My words remain in you,*
> *ask whatever you wish, and it will be given you* (John
> 15:7).

The conditions are that we abide and obey. The promise to the branches is that they are not limited to their own power. In the previous chapter we were promised,

> *If you ask me for anything in My name, and I will do*
> *it ... And I will ask the Father, and He will give you*
> *another Counselor to be with you forever—the Spirit*
> *of truth* (John 14:14,16,17).

To abide is the same as being controlled by the Spirit. If we are controlled by Him, we will want what He wants, therefore, it will be granted.

The ultimate purpose is to glorify the Father,

This is to my Father's glory, that you bear much fruit, showing yourselves to be My disciples (John 15:8).

This chapter shows a progression of fruit, *bear fruit* and *more fruitful* in verse 2 and *bear much fruit* in verse 5 and 8. The more fruit we bear, the more we glorify God.

The secret of obeying is loving

As the Father has loved Me, so have I loved you. Now remain in My love (John 15:9).

If we abide and obey, we will experience His love.

Christ loves us as much as the Father loved Him. How much does the Father love the Son?

I have given them the glory that You gave Me, that they may be one as we are one, I in them and You in me. May they be brought to complete unity to let the world know that you sent Me and have loved them even as you have loved Me (John 17:22-23).

God loves us as much as He loves His Son. Jesus wants us to experience the oneness that He experiences with the Father.

We will never be elevated to the godhead, but we can experience the same intimate relationship that the Godhead has.

My wife, Mary, and I went to see the daughter of a woman in our church. She had strayed so far that she was supporting a young man with a drug habit. We spent some time explaining the gospel and became convinced that she had made a decision for Christ, and even used to be active in a local church. Sin had so degraded her that she didn't think that God could ever love her. We had her read the above verse (John 17:23). She showed no emotion so Mary said, "Read it again." We had her read it 3 or 4 times and finally it gripped her and she broke down with tears streaming down her face.

She became so excited about the Lord that she almost got fired from her job the next day from sharing her faith so much. She could be found in our congregation every Sunday radiating Christ's love in her face. Read that verse until you are sure you understand it—it will change your life!

God gave the Son glory because He loved Him,

> *Father, I want those You have given Me to be with Me where I am and to see My glory, the glory You have given Me because You loved me before the creation of the world* (John 17:24).

Jesus shared His glory with believers because He loves us, *I have given them the glory that You gave Me* (John 17:22). How did Christ share His glory with us?

1. We are partakers of His divine nature (2 Peter 1:4).
2. We are unconditionally accepted in the Beloved One (Ephesians 1:6).
3. He *raised us up with Christ and seated us with Him in the heavenly realms* (Ephesians 2:6).
4. We are sealed with the Holy Spirit until the day of redemption (Ephesians 4:30).

5. We will judge the world and angels (1 Corinthians 6:2,3).

6. We *will reign with Him for a thousand years* (Revelation 20:6).

7. We *are heirs—heirs of God and co-heirs with Christ, if indeed we share in His sufferings in order that we may also share in His glory* (Romans 8:17).

8. Christ, who spoke and created the whole universe and upholds it by the Word of His power shares everything with us, *All are yours, and you are of Christ, and Christ is of God* (1 Corinthians 3:22,23). The godhead shares everything with believers.

9. *The creation waits in eager expectation for the sons of God to be revealed* (Romans 8:19).

10. In the future, He will reveal His glory in us, *I consider that our present sufferings are not worth comparing with the glory that will be revealed in us* (Romans 8:18).

The climax of human history will usher in His glory revealed in His saints. Now we are to reflect the Lord's glory in our lives,

> *And we, who with unveiled faces all reflect the Lord's glory, are being transformed into His likeness with ever-increasing glory, which comes from the Lord, Who is the Spirit* (2 Corinthians 3:18).

Until then we are to remain in His love,

> *even as I have obeyed my Father's commands remain in His love* (John 15:10).

The pattern of Christ's life was to obey and love the Father.

Love is not a sentiment; divine love comes from the very nature of God and is an irresistible power. If we abide in the vine, love will flow through us because it is the very nature of His life. Radium must be enclosed in lead to keep it from radiating away because that is its nature. We don't have to try to manufacture God's love; it will naturally flow from Christ living in us.

The secret of loving is joy

> *I have told you this so that My joy may be in you and that your joy may be complete* (John 15:11).

How can I be a happy Christian? His life is joy and you can't have real joy without His life. To experience it we must abide, obey, love; and then we will have His joy. And His joy doesn't depend on circumstances,

> *who for the joy set before Him endured the cross, scorning its shame, and sat down at the right hand of the throne of God* (Hebrews 12:2).

How could Jesus experience joy while enduring the excruciating pain and shame of the cross? Because He had an eternal perspective; He looked forward to having you and I and multitudes enjoy eternity with Him.

There is a difference between fun and joy. Say the two words, fun and joy. When you say fun, it is just a shallow, short burst of breath and it's gone. But when you say joy, it comes deep from within and requires a long exhaling of breath. Circumstances can bring a short burst of joy and then vanish forever. However, real joy is deeply satisfying and is lasting.

Joy comes from knowing that God takes great delight in us,

> *He will take great delight in you, He will quiet you with His love, He will rejoice over you with singing* (Zephaniah 3:17).

Take a while to meditate on that picture; God delighting in you, quieting you with His love and singing over you. I know, it's hard to believe but God's Word says it, so believe it!

Salvation brings fellowship and joy with God,

> *That which we have seen and heard declare we unto you that you also might have fellowship with us and truly our fellowship is with the Father and with His Son, Jesus Christ. And these things write I unto you, that your joy may be full* (1 John 1:3-4).

Joy comes from knowing Christ because joy is one of the fruit of the Spirit (Galatians 5:22). Fellowship with God results in a joyful Christian,

> *...be filled* (controlled) *with the Spirit. Speak to one another with psalms, hymns, and spiritual songs. Sing and made music in your heart to the Lord* (Ephesians 5:18).

Just as God rejoices in singing over us; fellowship with Him causes us to sing over Him. True Christianity is joy and should be the everyday life of a believer.

We may suffer grief in this life called *the vale of tears,* but, like Jesus on the cross, we can have a deep joy when we compare it to eternity,

In this you greatly rejoice, though now for a little while you may have had to suffer grief in all kinds of trials. These have come so that your faith—of greater worth than gold, which perishes even though refined by fire—may be proved genuine and may result in praise, glory, and honor when Jesus Christ is revealed. Though you have not seen Him, you love Him; and even though you do not see Him now, you believe in Him and are filled with an inexpressible and glorious joy (1 Peter 1:6-8).

As the song writer wrote, *It will be worth it all when we see Jesus.*

The secret of joy is knowing.

There is a progression of knowing Christ more intimately portrayed as a friend in John 15. Verse 13 and 14 says,

Greater love has no one than this, that he lay down his life for his friends. You are my friends if you do what I command.

And verse 15 states,

I no longer call you servants, because a servant does not know his master's business. Instead, I have called you friends, for everything that I learned from My Father I have made known to you.

A master doesn't tell a servant everything, but he shares everything with a friend. Abraham was called *a friend of*

God. Some believers have a more intimate relationship with Christ than others.

Jesus said,

> *For I gave them the words you gave Me and they accepted them. They knew with certainty that I came from You, and they believed that You sent Me* (John 17:8).

Jesus preached in parables to the multitudes, but He then would take His disciples aside and share the secret meaning of the parables to them. Friendship delights in fellowship, counsel, and you trust them with things that you would not share with others.

The secret of joy is knowing Christ more intimately; the more we know and obey Him, the greater our joy. Jesus said,

> *Whoever has My commands and obeys them, He is the one who loves Me and will be loved by My Father, and I, too, will love him and show Myself to him* (John 14:21).

There is a progression: the more we know Him, the more we love Him; the more we love Him, the more we will obey Him, and He will respond by showing more of Himself to us. This process is an ever deepening, endless cycle that progressively draws us closer to Him.

The end purpose of abiding, obeying, loving, and having joy is that we might bear fruit,

> *You did not choose me, but I chose you and appointed you to go and bear fruit—fruit that will remain* (John 15:16).

Only work done by Christ working through us will remain. All of man's works in the flesh will wilt and die. They will be judged as *wood, hay, and stubble* that are burned up at the Judgment Seat of Christ.

The more we abide, the more we will realize our purpose for living with eternities values in mind. Let someone else drill the oil wells and build the skyscrapers, we can impact lives that will live for all eternity.

In the book *Hudson Taylor's Spiritual Secret*, he tells how that for years as a missionary in China he exhausted himself trying to do God's work. After he learned how to abide as a branch and draw life giving sap out of the vine, he wrote to his sister in 1869:

> *I knew that if only I could abide in Christ, all would be well, but I could not. The more he tried to get in the more he found himself slipping out, so to speak, the light finally dawned. Here I feel is the secret; not asking how I am to get sap out of the vine and into myself, but remembering that Jesus is the vine, the root, the stem, branches, twigs, leaves, flowers and fruit—I do not have to make myself a branch. The Lord Jesus tells me I am a branch, I am part of Him; and I have to just believe it and act upon it. I have seen it long enough in the Bible, but I believe it now as a living reality. I do not know how far I may be able to make myself intelligible about it, for there is nothing new or strange or wonderful—and yet all is new! In a word, Whereas once I was blind, now I see ... I am dead and buried with Christ—aye, and risen too and ascended ... God reckons me so, and tells me to reckon myself so. He knows best. Oh, the joy of seeing this truth—I pray that the eyes of your understanding*

may be enlightened, that you may know and enjoy the riches freely given us in Christ.

He was paraphrasing,

I pray also that the eyes of your heart be enlightened in order that you may know the hope to which He has called you the riches of His glorious inheritance in the saints (Ephesians 1:18).

May you discover you riches in Christ and say, "I see it! It is nothing new, but now I see it!"

Chapter 9

IN CHRIST WE
KNOW GOD'S WILL

In a *Peanuts* comic strip, there was a conversation between Lucy and Charlie Brown. Lucy said that life is like a deck chair. Some place it so they can see where they are going; some place it so they can see where they have been; and some place it so they can see where they are at present. Charlie Brown's reply, "I can't even get mine unfolded."

Perhaps your life seems that way, confused and lacking direction. Life has thousands of decisions, major and minor. "How can I know God's will?" is one of the most often asked questions. Many Christians are frustrated and feel they are out of God's will because they are in a bad marriage, dissatisfied in their vocation, etc.

There are many questions about God's will: "What does God's will mean?" "Does God have a plan for my life?" "How can I discover God's will?" "How can I know God's will for sure in a specific situation?"

It is exciting to know that God has a perfect will for our lives, but we have to surrender and be transformed in our minds to know it,

> ...*be transformed by the renewing of your mind. Then you will be able to test and approve what God's will is—His good, pleasing, and perfect will* (Rom. 12:2).

Christ in You Is the Will of God.

Many envision God's will as something vague and mysterious. They discouragingly ask, "How am I going to make contact with this illusive will of God? They are always going, doing, agonizing over every decision; to buy a car, house, a different job, or a move. They are always *putting out the fleece* trying to discern what to do. They never think of God's will as something that is natural, easy, and ordinary.

United with Christ by His Holy Spirit, the believer is in a state of being—that is the will of God.

The will of God is not some elusive future thing that is always out of reach—it is now! It is an ever present, on-going process, wherever you are, whatever you are doing.

The will of God is not a thing, but the person of Christ. The will of God is in you because God is in you!

Where does God work to will and to act according to His good purpose?

> *...for it is God who works in you to will and to act according to His good purpose* (Philippians 2:13).

God is not some outward formula to be learned, but the indwelling Spirit of Christ. Our sensitivity to His leading is brought into sharp focus as we abide in Him, listen to His Word, and obey Him.

Jesus didn't say He was a map, but that he was the way,

I am the way and the truth and the life (John 14:6).

We do not need a map labeled the *will of God*. All we need to do is follow Him by yielding and obeying.

What does Jesus say He will do?

...He goes on ahead of them, and His sheep follow Him because they know His voice (John 10:4).

All we need to do is hear His voice and follow Him. The will of God is not just doing something or going someplace. It is enjoying Christ as the *Sabbath rest for the people of God* (Hebrews 4:9).

Real contentment is abiding in Christ. Paul said,

...for I have learned the secret to be content whatever the circumstances. I know what it is to be in need, and I know what it is to have plenty. I have learned the secret of being content in any and every situation (Philippians 4:11,12).

The secret of being content in any and every situation is enjoying the presence of Christ living in us! God's will is not just doing, going, having or not having, it is constantly enjoying His presence. We can be satisfied with Him in every situation.

Why could Paul be content in every situation? Because he had confidence in Christ,

I can do everything through Him who gives me strength (Philippians 4:13).

We are sufficient in Him. He is all we need—just follow Him, enjoy Him, and respond to Him! External legalism with its formulas leads to despair; grace leads to rest and righteousness.

Paul stated that,

> *the righteous requirements of the law might be fully met in us, who do not live according to the flesh but according to the Spirit* (Romans 8:4).

The moment we *abide in Christ*, or *walk in the Spirit*, it just happens.

A faith dependence on Him leads to activity in a natural way. It is not something we force.

For example, we don't have to try to love people, just let Christ in us love the unlovely.

Paul said that he no longer lived, but *Christ lives in me* (Galatians 2:20). Paul was not annihilated as a person. He still exercised his will. But he experienced the exciting adventure of responding to Christ who motivated and empowered him. Sometimes he was a tentmaker to pay his own way. Once he was forbidden to go to a mission field by the Holy Spirit. But we have no record that Paul was ever anxious about the will of God. He didn't have to constantly worry about "Shall I go there?" "Shall I do this?" "Shall I buy this?"

Paul did not have to strive to do the will of God. Christ was in him—who was the will of God. Paul did not have to try to be like Christ. Christ was being Himself in Paul. Paul just responded.

Whether you are a housewife, pastor, factory worker, or banker—you are in the will of God because God is in you. You do not have to agonize to find the will of God. Just enjoy a love relationship with Him and do the natural things He prompts you to do until Christ, *Who is your life* (Colossians 3:4) tells you otherwise.

Jesus is in us being Himself in the obvious, natural activities of our daily lives. If there is another path to take, He will put up a stop sign.

Grace always leaves you living naturally in His supernatural life—this is the normal Christian life!

If Paul had a desire to go to a certain place, he continued on naturally, unless he got a red light and the door was closed. When he wanted to visit Ephesus, the Spirit stopped him. He didn't feel stricken with guilt and say, "I missed God's will." The Spirit was just saying, "Not now." (On his third missionary journey Paul went to Ephesus.) Scripture doesn't record that Paul had a prayer meeting. He just went on to the next logical place. He did the natural thing until God showed him something unnatural—a man from Macedonia in a dream.

Spend time enjoying a love relationship with Christ, rather than striving and worrying about the future. Embrace life now, where you are. Christ is in you—Who is the will of God. God interrupted Paul's life while he was absorbed with Christ living in him, doing the natural thing at the time.

> *The Christian Herald once carried an article about a senior executive of a large bank in New York City. It told how he had risen to a place of prominence and influence. At first, he served as an office boy then one day the president of the company called him aside and said, 'I want you to come into my office and work with me each day.' The young man replied, 'But what could I do to help you, sir? I don't know anything about finances.' 'Never mind that. You just stay by my side and keep your eyes and ears open.' 'That was*

the most significant experience of my life.' Said the executive, 'Being with that wise man made me just like him. I began to do things the way he did, and that accounts for what I am today.'

— Anonymous

We don't have to *stay by his side and keep our eyes and ears open*—Christ dwells in us to do His will through us. All we have to do is to yield and obey.

Our bodies were designed to do the will of God before we were born.

The Psalmist said,

For you created my inmost being; you knit me together in my mothers womb (Psalm 139:13).

The Hebrew meaning is *embroidered* with different colors. In the womb, God planned for David to have specific gifts. His DNA structure was designed at birth.
    The Psalmist goes on to say,

All the days ordained for me were written in your book before one of them came to be (verse 16).

David's length of life and his purpose were planned in advance. Just like David, God has an intelligently designed purpose for our lives. We can fight against the way we were designed, but it will be like a horse trying to fly. Some people are leaders, others followers. Some are introverted, some extroverted. God gives opportunity for us to make independent decisions in many areas of our life, but it gives great comfort to know that He has a major purpose for our lives.

The prophet Jeremiah was set apart before birth,

> *Before I formed you in the womb I knew you* (chose), *before you were born I set you apart; I appointed you as a prophet to the nations* (Jeremiah 1:5).

The Apostle Paul was set apart before birth,

> *But when God, Who set me apart from birth and called me by His grace, was pleased to reveal His Son in me so that I might preach Him among the Gentiles...* (Galatians 1:15-16).

All believers were set apart before birth,

> *For He chose us in Him before the creation of the world to be holy and blameless in His sight* (Ephesians 1:4).

Why were we created?

> *For we are God's workmanship, created in Christ Jesus to do good works, which God prepared in advance for us to do* (Ephesians 2:10).

It is exciting that God has planned good works for us to do in advance. All we have to do is respond to His leading.

The believer's body is a perfect instrument for a ray of God's glory to shine through. God made each believer unique. You are one of a kind. You can dye your hair, have plastic surgery, but no one has your fingerprints or your DNA structure. You are one of a kind to let God's glory shine through. We are finite and can't reveal all the glory of an infinite God, but we can emit a ray, a facet. Silence, submission and awe are the proper response to this breathtaking privilege.

Christ in our body expresses God's will.

The *old man* we used to be was unsalvageable. There was nothing that God could rehabilitate; the *old man* had to be put to death. In Christ, the *old man* is finished,

> *for we know that our old self was crucified with Him so the body of sin might be done away with* (Romans 6:6).

The believer was united with Christ in His death, burial, and resurrection. Christ's life is now in you. You are a new person to be controlled by Him.

Christ wants our *body parts* so He can live His life through them,

> *offer the parts of your body to Him as instruments of righteousness* (Romans 6:13).

He wants to think through our minds, see with our eyes, hear with our ears, etc. He lives in our bodies to do His will.

A seeing-eye dog looks straight ahead and lets nothing distract him. He is like a horse with blinders. If we let God look through our eyes, we will not stray from His will. One believer sees a need and responds, others don't. Why? A missionary only sees his field, others don't. Why? Because Jesus was looking through their eyes, *for it is God who works in you to will and to act according to His good purpose* (Philippians 2:13).

God is using our bodies to do His will and purpose. All we need to do is listen to our *ought-tos*. Like a toothache of the heart, He will move us to *will and to act*. We only have to respond. We don't have to pursue it, but just follow as He motivates us to minister. God will give us the desire and power to do His will.

There is a synchronization of our wills with God's will that is impossible to distinguish. Paul said,

The life I live in the body, I live by faith in the Son of God (Galatians 2:20).

God did not make Paul a robot, or a puppet, mechanically doing His will. Paul had a will that had to respond to God's leading to be effective.

However, Paul also said, *I live by faith.* Saul, the strong-willed Pharisee, was no longer Paul (meaning *little*), but a Spirit-controlled apostle living by faith in Christ. He had the same personality, but now under different management. Christ was living in Paul using his personality to express God's will. God was initiating, Paul was responding. God's will in Paul was in concert with Paul's will as he lived a life of faith. Paul's life was one of adventure as he joyfully anticipated what would come to pass each day.

Being leads to doing. Christ living in us, using our personality. Hot water is neutral, but passing through a tea bag it expresses its flavor. The bag could contain poison and be fatal. The believer chooses to be controlled by Christ or the flesh. We can choose to have Christ live through us and express His life and power. Or we can live a fleshly life and spread its poison.

Defining God's Will

Now that we understand the simplicity of God's will— Christ living His life through us—let's see how Scripture defines God's will. Understanding Scripture will also fine-tune our ability to respond to Christ's leading in our lives. First, let's consider **two erroneous views**:

1. Fatalism—God is sovereign, He does what He wants to do and there is nothing I can do about it. I must passively lie down and let it happen. Tevye, in *Fiddler on the Roof,* asked "Would it upset some eternal plan, if I were a rich man?" Like Tevye, some believers respond to every circumstance with "Praise the Lord anyhow!" This is fatalistic passivism.

2. God has a selection of wills. There is the perfect will of God, and then the permissive will of God. If we miss His perfect will then we are relegated to His permissive will.

This view leads some believers to the quicksand mentality that they are always in the permissive will of God. They reason, "Since I have sinned and missed God's perfect will in the past, now I feel I'm forever relegated to His permissive will. However, I want to continue to seek His perfect will." They feel that they are continually out of God's perfect will because they fail constantly by sins of omission, commission, thought life, wrong decisions, etc.

Romans 12:2 calls God's will as, *good, pleasing and perfect will*. But I can't find one scripture that speaks of God's permissive will. If you find one, let me know. The word *permission* only occurs four times in 1 Corinthians 6:12 and 10:23 referring to the believer's liberty to make choices.

The term *permissive will of God* is not found in Scripture. It comes from human reasoning; "a holy God does not condone sin, so when we sin, we must be relegated to the permissive will of God. We are now in plan B, not plan A."

This has a subtle effect on our view of God's will. Some people may think that God's will becomes a mirage. It is just out ahead of us so we must continue to look, but never expect to find it. Others have found it, but they are still looking. Someday, some mystical light will shine, a warm tingly feeling will surge over us, and we will have found it. But until that time we must continue this frantic search that consumes us.

Legalism (externalism) uses this reasoning as a whip to keep us striving until we find it. "If you only dedicate yourself more, give yourself more to God, then you will know His perfect will." This error never allows the believer to enjoy living in the throbbing now. He is on a perpetual merry-go-round trying to grasp the golden ring that is always out of reach.

Many believers see themselves as just a housewife, office worker, etc., waiting for God's will. As a result, they are bored with what they are doing now. If the apostle Paul could enjoy God's will in prison, we can have joy now—right where we are!

There are three types of wills:

God's Sovereign Will is His plan for the universe that includes all history and eternity. Everything will eventually work out according to His will. He knows what nations will rise and how leaders will rule. No one can keep His sovereign will from being carried out.

No man can understand His sovereign plan,

> *Oh, the depth of the riches of the wisdom and knowledge of God! How unsearchable His judgments, and His paths beyond tracing out! Who has known the mind of the Lord? Or who has been His counselor?* (Romans 11:33,34).

God's sovereign will could also be called His "secret will" because it is only known to man as God chooses to reveal it.

All things work out in conformity with the purpose of His will,

> *In Him we were also chosen, having been predestined according to the plan of Him who works out everything in conformity with the purpose of His will* (Ephesians 1:11).

God planned in eternity past that Christ would die on the cross,

> *He was chosen before the creation of the world, but was revealed in these last times for your sake* (1 Peter 1:20).

God also knew that sinful men would be involved in His crucifixion,

This man was handed over to you by God's set purpose and foreknowledge; and you, with the help of wicked men, put Him to death by nailing Him to the cross (Acts 2:23).

God sovereignty was involved, because it happened according to His purpose and foreknowledge.

The latter part of this verse reveals that men have a free will and can make wrong choices. Wicked men crucified Christ. God never condones sin, but His sovereign will can mysteriously make the bad work together for good to accomplish His purpose.

God's sovereign, or *secret will,* cannot be understood until He reveals it. Even then, our finite minds cannot completely reconcile God's sovereignty with man's responsibility (or free will) completely.

God's sovereignty is not fatalism. Even though God mysteriously works man into His sovereign will to accomplish His eternal purposes, man is still a free moral agent who is allowed to make wrong choices.

An architect may plan a house. In the process of building the house, the carpenter may get drunk and ruin part of the structure. The architect may have to hire another man to restore and replace the damaged structure. There may be material shortages that cause delays, or natural disasters that destroy part or all of the building. But the architect works around all of these hindrances and finally completes the house that represents his intelligently designed purpose as outlined in his blueprints.

God told Abraham that his people would spend 400 years in a foreign land, but someday his descendants would return and claim the promised land. This decree of God came about through a complicated process.

Joseph's brothers sold him into slavery. This was a sinful act of their will and they were later held responsible for their moral actions. Joseph was falsely accused and put into prison. God used a complicated series of events, dreams, people, and circumstances to elevate Joseph to a place of leadership. However, the brothers' sin and intended harm was actually used by God for good and the saving of many lives. Joseph told his repentant brothers,

> *You intended to harm me, but God intended it for good*
> *to accomplish what is now being done, the saving of*
> *many lives"* (Genesis 50:20).

God's sovereign will cause mans evil acts to turn out for good in the end.

A man once boasted how he was acting voluntarily in courting his wife. It was his decision to propose. He initiated the relationship and was in control of the entire courtship. However, after they were married, his wife informed him how she wanted to marry him and moved to make him willing. She acted in subtle ways that a man wouldn't understand to entice him to the altar. She claimed to be the one who willed them to be married.

Likewise, God used many subtle ways to bring Joseph to a place of power in Egypt: dreams and their interpretation, circumstances, and people's wrong choices. The events no doubt influenced the decisions that men made, but they were still exercising their free will.

Another example would be how Jesus knew that Judas would betray Him, but Judas was responsible for his actions,

> *The Son of Man will go just as it is written about him.*
> *But woe to that man who betrays the Son of Man!*

It would be better for him if he had not been born
(Matthew 26:24).

The sovereign will of God includes everything that happens in the universe. It takes man's sins and wrong decisions and causes them to ultimately work out for God's glory. Man is not a puppet; he still makes choices, but a sovereign God determines the final outcome.

Scripture says,

Indeed Herod and Pontius Pilate met together with the Gentiles and the people of Israel in this city to conspire against your holy servant Jesus, whom you anointed. They did what your power and will had decided beforehand should happen (Acts.4:27,28).

Men conspired against Jesus what God decided beforehand would happen. Can we understand this? No! Our finite minds cannot think like God. We would not worship a God whose thoughts could be reduced to the limited thinking of our finite minds. However, both God's sovereignty and man's responsibility are taught side-by-side in Scripture; and both must be accepted as truth.

God's glory is not always manifested immediately, but it is certain. God's sovereign will now permits good and evil to work together. A Jesus and Judas, a Gabriel and Lucifer exist side by side. But Christ will defeat Satan forever, judge righteously and reign in glory for eternity.

We are told,

And we know that in all things God works for the good of those who love Him, who have been called according to His purpose (Romans 8:28).

It says that all things work together for good—not that all things are good.

Verse 29 says that they all work together to conform believers to Christ. A flat tire, a crying child, a leaky roof all work together for good. The mature saint may not understand, but he can trust that his trials are part of the sovereign plan of an all-wise and loving God.

> *We are told that* all things work together for good — *those are the pieces.* To those called according to God's purpose—*that is the picture. Whether or not we let God assemble the pieces determines whether it shall be a picture or only a puzzle. Are you perplexed and frustrated over this event or that happening in your life? Do not take it out of God's hand to work it into your design. God saw the picture from the start and you don't see it yet and won't until it is finished.*
> —Vance Havner, *Hope Thou In God.*

The Apostle Paul could not understand God's ways,

> *How unsearchable His judgments, and His paths beyond tracing out! Who has known the mind of the Lord? Or who has been His counselor?* (Romans 11:33,34).

He also proclaimed,

> *And He made known to us the mystery of His will* (Ephesians 1:9).

God's will is *secret* or a *mystery* until He reveals it to us. We cannot fathom how God blends good and evil together to accomplish His eternal purpose, but it does provide great comfort during trials.

God's Moral Will as revealed in scripture teaches men how to live. These truths impact our lives, but may not directly determine every decision we make in life (e.g. vocation, marriage, where to live, what we wear, or eat, etc.)

There is no difference between Scripture (the written Word) and Christ (the Living Word); they are both a revelation of God's will. Throughout the New Testament, *The Word of the Lord* is used to describe the disciple's preaching as being a message from the Lord, delivered with His authority and made effective by His power.

Paul said,

> *All Scripture is God-breathed, and is useful for teaching, rebuking, correcting and training in righteousness, so the man of God may be thoroughly equipped for every good work* (2 Timothy 3:16).

All Scripture is a revelation of God's will and contains all man needs to be equipped for life. His Word contains 100 percent of God's moral will. Decisions that contradict Scripture are never consistent with God's will.

Man's Free Will is the freedom God has given man to make choices. There is a danger in thinking that God has a specific, perfect individual will for each person that covers every minute, detailed area of our lives: what we wear, eat, where we go, our job, the house we buy, etc. This paralyzes the believer into inactivity. He fossilizes, hesitating to make any decision for fear of missing God's will.

Then, when he does act, he suffers guilt wondering if he has missed God's will. He feels guilty on two counts: First, of not listening to God's signals. Secondly, when he does act, he has missed God's will. In this spiritual strait-jacket, a believer could take all day making simple decisions like what to eat or wear. Satan works overtime to paralyze the believer with guilt to rob him of his joyous freedom in Christ. The believer then lives in constant floating guilt, fearing that he is out of God's will.

The liberty we have in Christ gives us great freedom to make a multitude of decisions in our personal life, as long as they do not violate God's moral will revealed in Scripture. We are faced with making many decisions not specifically mentioned in Scripture. However, the Holy Spirit will provide wisdom and discernment in making these decisions without restricting us with puppet-like actions. Spiritual maturity will motivate us to make these decisions so they will glorify God.

God told Adam,

> You are free to eat from any tree in the garden; but you must not eat from the tree of knowledge of good and evil, for when you eat of it you will surely die (Genesis 2:16-17).

Verse 9 says *the Lord God made all kinds of trees.* God told Adam he was *free to eat* of any tree except one—the one He prohibited.

God did not design the first man as a robot; he had great latitude for making decisions—as long as they did not violate God's moral will. Adam probably had a delightful time anticipating which of the delicious fruits he would have for dinner. No matter which one he chose, he couldn't miss God's will.

If a parent says to his son, "Johnny, you can go outside and play, but don't go out of the yard." This privilege both assumes and restricts his freedom. He can enjoy many activities: run, sit, sleep, play games, etc. Whatever he does in the yard is within the parent's will. Likewise, God has given us great liberty to enjoy free choices in most areas of our lives—as long as it is within His moral will.

An anonymous writer said,

A little boy was riding his tricycle furiously around the block over and over again. Finally a policeman stopped and asked him why he was going around and around. The boy said that he was running away from home. Then the policeman asked why he was just going around the block. The boy responded, 'Because my mom said that I'm not allowed to cross the street.'

As in non-moral decisions, the believer's aim is to glorify and please God. Our ability to do this will be sharpened by wisdom and discernment derived from Scripture which, in turn, will enhance our sensitivity to the leading of the Holy Spirit.

God's *perfect will* is always in harmony with His moral will and brings joy and spiritual blessing to the believer. When someone speaks of being in the center of God's will, we might picture each specific decision as being made in a circle encompassing God's moral will. When a believer makes a decision that is outside of God's moral will, some call this God's second best or God's permissive will. However, it is never God's will that the believer sin, regardless of the labels we put on our actions. Sin is never condoned and has disastrous consequences. However, God always allows us to exercise our free will and may later use it as a learning tool to shape our lives for greater fruitfulness.

Joseph's brothers violated God's moral will when they sold him into slavery, but God's sovereign will, mysterious and hidden, used both good and evil to accomplish His plan.

God's moral will, revealed by the Holy Spirit through Scripture, should always be compatible with God's individual will for every day decisions in our lives. However, God's sovereign will can use evil acts and foolish decisions that will ultimately glorify Him.

Scripture makes it clear that:

1. God's moral will, revealed in the Word by commands and principles, is to be obeyed;

2. Where the Bible gives no direction in non-moral decisions, the believer is free to make his own choices;

3. These should be wise decisions motivated by the desire to glorify God.

The vast universe is an illustration of God's sovereign will. The inanimate objects hurling through space in an orderly fashion conform to God's laws of nature. They do not have will and thus do not make decisions. However, man, apart from angels, is the only creature which has a will to discern God's will.

A king may have a sovereign will for his kingdom while allowing his subjects to exercise their free wills in many things with diversity and a sense of freedom. The king does not legislate and control every activity of his people. That would make them slaves or robots. But the king's subjects look to him for leadership and protection. The King of kings exercises His sovereign will for our lives while allowing us the exercise of our free wills in vast areas of our lives.

Many people think that freedom is the license to do whatever they want, but true freedom is the ability to do what you know is right. It takes obedience in order to have true freedom. I can sit at a piano and be free to play any keys that I want, but I don't have freedom, because I can't play anything but noise. It takes years of practice and obedience to lesson plans in order to be truly free at the piano, and then you can play all kinds of music.

Chapter 10

IN CHRIST WE
DISCERN GOD'S WILL

Two professors were arguing about the Bible. One said, "Bet you don't even know the Lord's prayer?" "Everyone knows that, "Now I lay..." "Gosh, I didn't realize you knew the Bible!" Few have the basic truth needed to discern God's will.

Once we are in Christ, we are admonished to

live by the Spirit and you will not gratify the desires of the flesh (Galatians 5:16).

Jesus said that, *His sheep follow Him because they know His voice* (John 10:4). But we must know His voice and be sensitive to it. How can we refine our ability to respond to His leading? There are several things we can do to *know His voice* and respond.

Learn His Word. All Scripture is related to Christ

And beginning with Moses and all the Prophets, He explained to them what was said in all the Scriptures concerning Him (Luke 24:17).

And we are told

In the beginning was the Word, and the Word was with God, and the Word was God (John 1:1).

Christ is called the *Word*. God doesn't separate Christ in us, the Living Word, from the written word. If we want to recognize the voice of the Living Word, we must learn of Him through the written word.

The authority of Scripture is the authority of Jesus Christ; they are indivisible. To attempt to distinguish the two is like asking which blade of a pair of scissors is more important, or which leg of a pair of pants is more necessary. We know Christ through the Bible, and we understand the Bible through the knowledge of Christ; the two cannot be separated. That is why Paul calls it the Word of Christ.
—Ray Steadman, *Sermon on Ephesians 6:14-17).*

God's Word may not tell us how to make every specific individual decision in our lives, but it does reveal God's moral will. And many of its commands and principles relate to specific decisions we have to make.

Hundreds of flesh and blood illustrations of men and women who made good and bad decisions, along with the consequences, are recorded in scripture. The Holy Spirit can illuminate our minds and give us wisdom and discernment to use scripture to make decisions compatible with God's will.

As we know the mind of Christ by knowing His Word, we will make right decisions.

All scripture is inspired by God and profitable to prepare the believer for every good work,

All Scripture is God-breathed and is useful for teaching, rebuking, correcting, and training in righteousness, so that the man of God may be thoroughly equipped for every good work (1 Timothy 3:16-17).

Therefore Paul challenged believers to

Do your best to present yourself to God as one approved, a workman who does not need to be ashamed and who correctly handles the word of truth (2 Timothy 2:15).

One hundred percent of God's moral will is revealed in His Word. Therefore, if we are to know God's will, we must know His Word. His Will and Word are inseparable.

No prayers of guidance are needed in areas where God has already spoken. The immutable God of the universe won't change His attributes, plans, or purposes. He is not a fickle God who will change His mind.

Subjective guidance in ways that contradict God's Word can be destructive. We cannot say, "The Spirit led me" when it contradicts His Word. The Holy Spirit who inspired men to record the Father's will can never lead His children contrary to what He has written.

Learn to Live by the Spirit.

Many quote the Lord's prayer in Luke 11:2-4 for guidance today. But it was written before the New Covenant that was instituted after Jesus death. Later in the chapter Luke added,

If you then though you are evil, know how to give good gifts to your children, how much more will your

Father in Heaven give the Holy Spirit to those who ask Him! (v. 13).

The Holy Spirit was sent at Pentecost (Acts 2:1-4). He now indwells every believer at the time of the new birth (1 Corinthians 12:13). We now *live by the Spirit* (Galatians 5:16). Christ, Who is our life (Colossians 3:4), now dwells in us providing daily guidance.

Grace always leaves us living naturally in His supernatural life.

Notice that most of the references of the Holy Spirit's leading listed in this section refer to our spiritual life and not specific decisions concerning the mundane things of life. These scriptures refer to wisdom and understanding that will allow us to make decisions that will glorify God in our lives.

We are told that

those who are led by the Spirit of God are sons of God (Romans 8:14).

In this chapter, the Spirit is leading the believer to moral victory in the Spirit rather than defeat in the flesh (verse 13) and the witness of sonship (verse 15). There is no promise of specific answers to every decision in life. God's main concern is that our lives glorify Him.

Paul reminds believers

But if you are led by the Spirit, you are not under law (Galatians 5:18).

Again the word *led* does not necessarily refer to specific individual decisions, but an overall response to the Spirit's prompting rather than being under the law. Being led by the Spirit results in the fruit of the Spirit (verses 22,23) in contrast to the acts of the flesh (verses 19-21). The issue is how to have continuous victory over the flesh. The Lord's main concern is that we manifest the fruit of the Spirit in our home, vocation, recreation, etc. so that we may glorify Him in every area of our lives.

In Ephesians, Paul says

Therefore do not be foolish, but understand what the Lord's will is (5:17).

We do this by being *filled* (controlled) *by the Spirit* (verse 18). Being controlled by the Spirit is imperative if we are to know God's will. The effect of being controlled by the Spirit is joyful spiritual singing (verse 19), giving of thanks (verse 20), and mutual subjection (verse 21). This submission is then applied to relationships in the home and vocation (5:22-6:9).

The Holy Spirit is a person and speaks to us personally. However, just as it is impossible to explain our salvation experience to unbelievers, likewise it is impossible to describe the subjective leading of the Spirit. Paul said, *For Christ's love compels us* (2 Corinthians 5:14). There is a *still small voice* inaudible to human ears that speaks to our heart. This is the Spirit Himself who

testified with our spirit that we are God's children (Romans 8:16).

We are told to

Let the peace of God rule in your hearts (Colossians 3:15).

Rule means to be an umpire. Peace functions as an umpire that *calls* each decision in question. When the believer is controlled by the Spirit he experiences an inner peace that *transcends understanding* (Philippians 4:7). This peace is like an umpire calling us *Safe!* Like the peaceful calm in the center of a hurricane, we experience peace in the center of His will. Someone has aptly said, "If in doubt, don't."

Led of the Spirit refers primarily to the joyful, spirit-controlled life. It is not a promise that God will act as an umpire in every decision of life. It describes a life that is totally dependent on the Holy Spirit.

There are many non-moral decisions where Christians lack peace. There is often a *lack of peace* for nervous grooms when they face the important step in marriage. There wouldn't be many marriages if weddings were called off just because of anxious grooms.

There will always be agreement between God's Word, the inward guidance of the Holy Spirit, and circumstances when trying to discern God's will in the storms of life.

A young girl once counseled with her pastor, Dr. Lehman Strauss, about marrying a young man. After a short discussion, it became evident that the young man was not a believer and unsuitable as a husband. Dr. Strauss asked, "Why do you think you should marry this young man?" She replied, "The Spirit told me." To which Dr. Strauss replied, "Which spirit?"

We are told that a believer is to be *filled with the Spirit* in Ephesians 5:18; and that he is to, *Let the Word of Christ dwell in you richly* in Colossians 3:16. The Word and the Spirit of Christ are synonymous. The Living Word, Christ, and the written word, Scripture, are both expressions of God's will. Christ is in us, through the Holy Spirit. The more we master the written word, the more sensitive we will be to the Living Word Who dwells within.

I read a story about an aged lighthouse keeper who had been on the job more than 20 years. At his lighthouse, a gun was set to go off every hour to warn the ships. Year after year, the keeper had heard the blast of the shotgun on the hour throughout the day and night. Then the inevitable happened. Something went wrong with the mechanism in the middle of the night and the gun did not go off. It is reported that the startled keeper became fully awake, and said, "What was that?" The absence of the sound when he should have heard it alarmed him as much as the presence of the sound would have startled someone not accustomed to it.

A believer *keeping in step with the Spirit* (Galatians 5:25), *abiding in Christ* (John 15:7), will develop a sensitivity to the Spirit's leading in all things.

Learn to Interpret Circumstances.

Circumstances are the least reliable in discerning God's will. However, God does, in His providence, control circumstances. God can open and close doors.

The Apostle Paul told the church at Antioch,

> *On arriving there they gathered the church together and reported all that God had done through them and how he had opened the door of faith to the Gentiles* (Acts 14:27).

He also said,

> *Now when I went to Troas to preach the gospel of Christ and found that the Lord had opened a door for*

me (2 Corinthians 2:12). But he added, *I still had no peace of mind ... So I said good-bye to them and went on to Macedonia* (verse 13).

Opportunities do not guarantee tranquility and peace. Paul often confronted opposition and trials along with spiritual victories. Paul did not take advantage of this open door; he left Troas to go look for Titus. Paul bypassed this opportunity for a more pressing matter. Paul did not consider walking past an open door of opportunity a rejection of God's will. Some think Paul returned later and established a church in Troas which he later visited while passing through (Acts 20:6)

To assume that an open door is absolute proof of God's will could be misleading. If a pastor has several churches showing interest in him, which one is God's will? It would take wisdom and discernment to determine the right one. Circumstances alone can't be the only criteria for discerning God's will.

Many believers extend a lot of effort to interpret circumstances as they relate to dating, money, jobs, homes, etc. However, this is not the Biblical pattern. Paul didn't care whether he made tents, lived from offerings, or was in prison. His only concern was that *Christ might be preached* (Philippians 1:18).

The book of Acts throbs with persecution and martyrdom, but believers had one concern, proclaiming the gospel, not their safety. When persecution came they prayed,

Now, Lord, consider their threats and enable Your servants to speak Your Word with great boldness (Acts 4:29).

Many believers want a sign from God in order to know His will; like Gideon putting out the fleece to determine God's will. However, a closer look reveals some interesting insights. In Judges 6, an angel told Gideon that he would defeat Israel's enemy, Midian (verses 11-16). In response to Gideon's request for a confirming sign, God consumed his offering by fire (verses 17-24). The Spirit came upon Gideon, enabling him to marshal troops (verses 33-35). He then asked for two signs involving the fleece (verses 36-40). The Lord answered his request and gave him a miraculous victory (Judges 7).

Gideon's putting out the fleece was not a request to know God's will, but rather an expression of unbelief. Gideon already knew God's directions (Judges 6:37). In addition, he received several supernatural demonstrations; the angel claimed to be God (verse 21); his offering was consumed by fire (verse 21); God spoke to him (verses 23-26); and the Spirit of God came upon him for power (verse 34).

Gideon was not seeking a directional sign, but a miraculous one to prop up his weak faith. He was not obtaining guidance, but strengthening his faith to do the clear will of God which had already been given to him.

There is no teaching or example under the New Covenant given to encourage believers to imitate Gideon's method.

But some believers still cite Gideon's example and *put out the fleece*. But remember that Gideon did it to strengthen his weak faith, not to seek God's will. This misuse of Scripture raises some questions. How can a person find God's will by disobeying it and *putting out the fleece*?

The Old Covenant believers were not indwelled with the Holy Spirit. God does control circumstances, but great care should be used in asking for signs instead of using His normal methods.

> *A ship was fighting rough seas as it approached the narrow entrance to a harbor. A nervous passenger asked the calm and relaxed Captain, "Sir, how do you know when to guide the ship into the harbor entrance?" The captain pointed to the dark shore punctured with random dots of lights. "Do you see those three brightest lights there on the land?" The passenger searched for a moment, then nodded. "I have learned to steer my ship parallel to the shore until those three lights all line up as one. When the three lights agree, then I know that I can guide my ship safely into the narrow entrance of the harbor."*
>
> —Anonymous

In the storms of life, we must be sure three direction finders line up before moving on: the Word, the Holy Spirit, and circumstances. However, God has given us several additional helps to discern His will.

Learn to Pray in the Spirit.

We are to *live by the Spirit* (Galatians 5:16). Our whole life is lived in the sphere of the Spirit because Christ is our life. The normal Christian life is not **doing**, but **being**. As we concentrate on enjoying the life we have in Christ, He will direct what we do.

We are told to

> *build yourselves up in your most holy faith and pray in the Holy Spirit* (Jude 20).

We are told to *pray continually* (1 Thessalonians 5:17). How can we do that?

We are in Christ and He is in us; we are bone of His bone and flesh of His flesh. We are inseparable. We continually breathe and our heart continually beats without our conscious help. They are part of our life source. Our sub-conscious mind keeps them functioning.

If *Christ is our life,* we are to be to be continually controlled by Him and depending on Him through prayer even though we are not always conscious of it. Praying should be as natural as breathing.

My wife and I are soul-mates—God's Word says that we are *one flesh.* I'm not always conscious of her presence, but I sense our oneness even when we are apart. I don't make any decision without having deference to her. We enjoy sharing experiences in our lives. It is impossible to think of my life as separate from her.

That is the way our relationship should be with Christ. We are always conscious of Him even when we are not praying or meditating. We don't make any decisions without having deference to Him. We share all of our joys and sorrows with Him. It should be impossible to think of our life as separate from Him.

Christ is our life as we *abide in Him* and *walk in the Spirit* we will want what He wants. Our greatest satisfaction in life will be to glorify Him by doing His will. Our prayers will be a sensitive, intimate dialogue with our heavenly Father as He guides and empowers us in one triumphant spiritual victory after another. Our finite personal agenda will pale in significance as He uses us to accomplish His will. Our greatest concern will not be to get our prayers answered, but whether we are in concert with His exciting plan for our life.

A high school orchestra was preparing for a concert that featured a piano rendition of Greig's concert in A Minor No. 1. Before the performance, it was customary for the orchestra to tune up with an "A" sounded by the oboe player. The oboist, however, was a practical joker, and he had tuned his instrument a half step higher than the piano. You can imagine the effect. After the pianist played a beautiful introduction, the members of the orchestra joined in. What confusion! Every instrument was out of tune with the piano.

If our life is confusion, we need to get in tune with the Master conductor.

Prayer is vital to communication. If a husband and wife never talked to each other, how can they know what the other one is thinking? All the sermons, books, tapes, seminars and formulas on the will of God will not replace prayer. We cannot know God's will without prayer.

If we are *abiding in Christ*, God can give us what we want, because we will want what He wants,

> *If you remain in Me and My words remain in you, ask whatever you wish, and it will be given you* (John 15:7).

He promises that we can have confidence that our prayers will be answered,

> *This is the confidence we have in approaching God, that if we ask anything according to His will He hears us. And if we know that He hears us—whatever we ask—we know that we have what we asked of Him* (1 John 5:14-15).

Prayer is not telling God what to do, but getting into harmony with the omnipotent (all powerful), omniscient (all knowing) God of the universe. If we are to enjoy His *good and acceptable and perfect will* in our lives, we must be sensitive to His voice.

We aren't wise enough to always know what to ask for, but He does. Paul wrote,

> *Oh, the depth of the riches of the wisdom and knowledge of God! How unsearchable His judgments, and His paths beyond tracing out! Who has known the mind of the Lord? Or who has been His counselor?* (Romans 11:33-34).

Who has the audacity to give counsel to such a God!

In 1980, a Phoenix, Arizona Savings and Loan Company spent $400,000 trying to predict the future so they could make better business decisions. By 1994, most Phoenix Savings and Loan Companies were no longer in business. The believer has the advantage of asking guidance of the God who knows all things from the beginning and only desires what is best for us.

Shallow prayer asks God to pamper our wants; Spiritual prayer asks to see the big picture—how can we glorify God in our lives?

Two Christian men lived near each other. The first was a farmer. That year there had not been any rain for several weeks. One morning he got up and prayed for rain, but there was no rain that day. His next door neighbor was also up early, but he was praying that it would not rain. He was taking an unsaved friend fishing that morning. God hears both requests, but He can't answer both. He will do that which glorifies Him most.

God promises that we can

have confidence before God and receive from Him
anything we ask, because we obey His commands and
do what pleases Him (1 John 3:21-22).

God promises to

equip you with everything good for doing His will,
and may He work in us what is pleasing to Him,
through Jesus Christ, to whom be glory for ever and
ever, Amen" (Hebrews 13:21).

Notice that God says *for doing His will.* He then works, *in us what is pleasing to Him.* And finally, He gets the *glory.*

Grace is consistent: God initiates, directs, and empowers; we respond and get the blessing, but God gets the glory.

Many turn this around, they make their plans and then expect God to make them work out and they get the glory. Prayer is asking God to equip us for doing His will so that God may work in us what is pleasing to Him so that He may be glorified.

In Jesus' agony, His personal desires were submissive to a greater plan that would glorify the Father,

My Father, is it is not possible for this cup to be
taken away unless I drink it, may Your will be done
(Matthew 26:42).

As the Holy One, who had never known sin throughout eternity, contemplated becoming sin for us, His soul was traumatized,

My soul is overwhelmed with sorrow to the point of death (verse 38).

In such intense agony His sweat became drops of blood. Yet he still subjected His will to the Father's and added the disclaimer, *Yet not as I will, but as You will.*

The Apostle Paul said,

> *To keep me from becoming conceited because of these surpassing great revelations, there was given to me a thorn in my flesh, a messenger of Satan, to torment me. Three times I pleaded with the Lord to take it away from me. But He said to me, 'My grace is sufficient for you, for My power is made perfect in weakness.' Therefore I will boast all the more gladly about my weaknesses, so that Christ's power may rest on me* (2 Corinthians 12:7-9).

It is natural and proper to cry out to God to change our circumstances—but only if we add, *Yet not as I will, but as You will.* Paul gladly accepted his physical illness *so that Christ's power* would rest on him. He saw the bigger picture how God was using his circumstances to use him in a greater way for His glory.

Many Christians have faces so long they could eat oatmeal out of a quart milk bottle. Under the bondage of legalism they picture God as a tyrant, standing over them with a club, just waiting for them to make one mistake so He can bop them. They live in constant dread that one sin, or not performing, will result in a loss of job, their children will get sick, etc.

One unbeliever said, "I don't want to become a Christian because there are so many unhappy ones." What a twisted view of the *good, acceptable will of God.* There is joy, blessing, adventure, and fulfillment in living a life in concert with a loving, all knowing God.

God knows the deepest longings of our heart and satisfies them. The Psalmist said

> *Delight yourself in the Lord and He will give you the desires of your heart* (Psalm 37:4).

If we delight ourselves in the Lord by enjoying a love relationship with Him, our desires will become His desires. We will become sensitive to His leading and automatically *keep in step with the Spirit* (*walk in the Spirit*). We will enjoy *abiding in Christ* thus allowing Him to express His life through our body.

The more we practice His presence, the more we will experience the reality that *He is our life,* and find great joy in doing His will.

> *When a child first starts to color, he has two problems. First, he might choose colors that are inappropriate. Second, once the colors are chosen, he has a difficult time keeping the colors within the boundary lines. As he matures and keeps on coloring, he learns to keep within the guidelines and to choose the appropriate colors, resulting in a satisfying picture.*
>
> *As children of our heavenly Father, our prayer life often resembles a child's coloring. At first, we don't know what to pray for nor do our prayers stay within the guidelines of His will. As we mature and continue praying, though, we pray for the right things and stay within His will, resulting in a satisfying prayer life."*
>
> —Anonymous

earthly people; men who live after the flesh. *The Jerusalem that is above* is a heavenly system and represents children of the promise; those who live by faith.

She (Jerusalem) is *our mother*, because Christ is seated there at the right hand of God. It is our capital, the seat of government, and the center of activities,

> *But our citizenship is in heaven. And we eagerly await a Savior from there, the Lord Jesus Christ* (Philippians 3:20).

> *Who has blessed us in the heavenly realms with every spiritual blessing in Christ* (Ephesians 1:3).

It is written of Abraham,

> *For he was looking forward to the city with foundations, whose architect and builder is God* (Hebrews 11:10).

Not only Abraham, but

> *All these people were still living by faith when they died. They did not receive the things promised; they only saw them and welcomed them from a distance. And they admitted that they were aliens and strangers on earth. People who say such things show that they are looking for a country of their own ... Instead, they were longing for a better country—a heavenly one, Therefore, God is not ashamed to be called their God, for He has prepared a city for them* (Hebrews 11:13-16).

Jesus comforted His disciples by stating,

> *I am going there to prepare a place for you, and if I go and prepare a place for you, I will come back and take you to be with Me that you also may be where I am* (John 14:2,3).

Mount Sinai, the earthly city Jerusalem, representing the law and is contrasted with Mount Zion, the heavenly Jerusalem, that represents grace,

> *You have not come to a mountain that can be touched and that is burning with fire; to darkness, gloom and storm; to a trumpet blast or to such a voice speaking words that those who heard it begged that no further word be spoken to them, because they could not bear what was commanded: 'If even an animal touches the mountain, it must be stoned' The sight was so terrifying that Moses said, 'I am trembling with fear'* (Hebrews 12:18-21).

The law was given on Mount Sinai to reveal to sinful man the absolute holiness of God. The law was not given to redeem men, but to condemn them.

But the believer is reminded,

> *But you have come to Mount Zion, to the heavenly Jerusalem, the city of the living God. You have come to thousands upon thousands of angels in joyful assembly, to the church of the firstborn, whose names are written in heaven. You have come to God, the judge of all men, to the spirits of righteous men made perfect, to Jesus the mediator of a new covenant, and*